EACHER GUIDE

Includes Stud...
Worksheet...

M000274869

3rd–6th Grade

History

🔑 Answer Key

America's Story 3

MASTER BOOKS
— CURRICULUM —

Author: Angela O'Dell
Master Books Creative Team:
Editor: Craig Froman
Design: Terry White
Cover Design: Diana Bogardus
Copy Editors:
Judy Lewis
Willow Meek
Curriculum Review:
Kristen Pratt
Laura Welch
Diana Bogardus

First printing: May 2017
Fifth printing: August 2020

ISBN: 978-0-89051-984-4
ISBN: 978-1-61458-588-6 (digital)

Unless otherwise noted, Scripture quotations are from the King James Version of the Bible.

Unless otherwise noted, all images are from istock.com, shutterstock.com, Library of Congress, and Wikimedia Commons. All images used under the Creative Commons Attribution-Share Alike 3.0 Unported license (CC-BY-SA-3.0) are noted; license details available at creativecommons.org/licenses/by-sa/3.0/, (CC BY-SA 2.0), (CC BY 2.5), CC BY-SA 4.0). Other photos are public domain (PD-US), (CC0 1.0), and (PD-Art).

Printed in the United States of America

Please visit our website for other great titles: www.masterbooks.com

Author Bio: As a homeschooling mom and author, **Angela O'Dell** embraces many aspects of the Charlotte Mason method yet knows that modern children need an education that fits the needs of this generation. Based upon her foundational belief in a living God for a living education, she has worked to bring a curriculum that will reach deep into the heart of home-educated children and their families. She has written over 20 books, including her history series and her math series. Angela's goal is to bring materials that teach and train hearts and minds to find the answers for our generation in the never-changing truth of God and His Word.

Using This Teacher Guide

Features: The suggested weekly schedule enclosed has easy-to-manage lessons that guide the reading, worksheets, and all reviews. The pages of this guide are perforated and three-hole punched so materials are easy to tear out, hand out, grade, and store. Teachers are encouraged to adjust the schedule and materials needed in order to best work within their unique educational program.

A Living History of Our World: Delve into this exciting and thought-provoking history course spanning the turn of the 20th century through the early 2000s! Employing both oral narration and writing, this course allows students to express their thoughts and ideas through different mediums, helping to solidify what they are learning. Activities include Map Adventures, journaling, Scriptures and quotes for copywork, hands-on projects, and sketching and coloring. An additional timeline project lets students construct a visual of the course of history.

🕐	**Approximately 45 minutes per lesson, five days a week**
🔑	**Includes answer keys for activity sheets and reviews**
✏️	**Activity sheets for each chapter**
📄	**Reviews are included to help reinforce learning and provide assessment opportunities**
🔄	**Designed for grades 3 to 6 in a one-year history course**

Course Objectives: Students completing this course will

- ✔ Become familiar with American history from the early 1900s to the 21st century.
- ✔ Study history using the Charlotte Mason education philosophy to learn through interaction and story elements that connect students emotionally through learning about America and its influence throughout the world.

- ✔ Develop comprehension through oral and written narration, and create memories through notebooking and hands-on crafts.
- ✔ Connect to the lessons, including elements of writing and drawing, special project pages, written narration pages, and timeline characters to help children narrate their way through history's story.

Course Description: This curriculum has two parts, which includes this Teacher Guide and the student book. There are 28 chapters and five built-in reviews, making it easy to finish in one school year. The activity pages are an assortment of Map Adventures, areas to write/journal, Scriptures and famous sayings for copywork, hands-on projects, and pictures to draw and color. There is also a timeline project, including simple instructions for completion.

Table of Contents

Supply List

What preparations do you need to make to get ready for a wonderful year of history?

Gather the following items to complete your student activity pages:

- ☐ Scissors
- ☐ Clear tape
- ☐ Glue
- ☐ Colored pencils, markers, and crayons
- ☐ Optional: a package of index cards (lined or unlined)
- ☐ Optional: a plastic or metal ring on which to place the timeline cards
- ☐ Hole punch
- ☐ Stapler
- ☐ Hole reinforcements
- ☐ Construction paper
- ☐ Optional: poster board
- ☐ Encyclopedias (books or CD-ROM)
- ☐ Old magazines for pictures
- ☐ Current world and U.S. maps (see pages 17 and 18 of this Teacher Guide)
- ☐ Ruler

Optional Artist Study supply list:

- ☐ white paper
- ☐ pencils
- ☐ stack of lightweight paper
- ☐ crayons, colored pencils, or markers to color
- ☐ graph paper
- ☐ plastic garbage bags
- ☐ tempera paint
- ☐ tablespoons
- ☐ small containers
- ☐ paintbrushes or sponges
- ☐ water

A Note from the Author

History with a flavor of the Charlotte Mason method...

This series is based upon the belief that we all learn better by making a connection that is deeper than memorizing the facts. Charlotte Mason taught that we all need heroes. We need someone to look up to, someone to admire and aspire to emulate. Children need to understand the overall flow of history without getting hung up on the pressure of memorizing dates and random facts for a test. They need to have their love of learning protected and nurtured. My advice to you is to look at this course as a giant tool box, full of a huge variety of helpful tools. You do not have to use every single tool for it to be effective. My goal in writing is to give you, the parent/teacher, a plethora of tools to teach each child.

You know your student better than anyone. Adjust according to age/ability and learning style. For example, if a third/fourth grade–age child enjoys the reading, but all of the notebook pages are too much, then please just read the story and let him or her do the journaling pages that fit his or her ability. Encourage and show your child by example to relax, invest, and enjoy the journey. The Teacher's Guide is not written in stone — use it the way you need! Flexibility is what makes a good curriculum.

Remember, we are learning more permanently and making lasting connections when we can relate to the life aspects of what we are learning.

May you see the Hand of God throughout all of history! —Angela O'Dell

Getting Started: On page 7, there is a teacher's bookmark. Cut it out on the dotted black line, fold it on the gray line so the writing is on the outside, cover it with contact paper, and use it to keep your place as you are reading through *A Living History of Our World, America's Story, Volume 3*. On one side is information about narration, and on the other is an encouraging word from me to you, one educator to another.

On pages 17 and 18, you will find two maps. There is a map of the world and one of the United States. Geography skills are directly connected with history, and doing them both together makes the picture clearer in the child's mind.

Included in this Teacher Guide:

- **A convenient Teacher Page** at the beginning of each chapter's worksheets and activities. This includes:

    o   Any notes to the instructor about the chapter's materials or focus (if needed)

    o   **Supply lists** for needed items

    o   Answers or insight for **oral narration answers**. These questions are found in the chapter narration breaks in the textbook.

        ▪   Teachers are encouraged to use the narration questions. Not only does it create a dialogue about the written material, it can also help the student learn to develop the skill of mentally arranging his or her thoughts and be able to give coherent answers. It also helps students who may be struggling with writing or needing additional review opportunities.

        ▪   We also encourage the teacher to use the **Ready to Explore** questions that begin each chapter of the **textbook**. They are meant to get the student thinking about the ideas that will be presented. The student should not be expected to answer questions correctly when first presented with them at the start of the chapter. The teacher may use them to start a conversation about what the student already knows or thinks. The answers are given at the end of the chapter in the **textbook**. When the student has completed the chapter, it is a good time to ask the student the Ready to Explore questions again. The student will enjoy seeing how much he or she has learned.

- o   Optional ideas for additional study
- o   Suggested reading or supplemental books
- o   **Written narration** idea for older students (on the back of the page)

- **Draw/write pages**: These are pages that have journaling lines and spaces to draw (or paste pictures) in. On many of these pages, there are copywork sections and/or pictures to color.

  - o   Vocabulary component: Each chapter in the student **textbook** includes a specific word and definition highlighted in a blue background. Often on the activity sheets, the student is asked if he or she found the word and understand its definition. Other spaces are provided for the student to choose other words he or she has learned from the chapter and to show an understanding of the meanings of them as well.

  - o   Map component: A variety of maps are included in the activity sheets as both a geography and critical thinking application.

- **Answer Keys** for special exercises and course reviews (page **285**).

- **Glossary and Geographical Terms**: These are the featured word from each chapter as well as a handy list of geographical terms in a helpful list (page **309**).

- **Review Sheets:** Review sheets are included as part of the course. These can be used as a fun review option or even as unique graded tests on the material depending on the needs of your education program or student (page **269**). You also have the option to allow him or her to do open book reviews or assessments depending the skill level of your student.

- **Special-project pages:** Also scattered through the Teacher Guide are mini-project pages. These will involve cut-and-glue projects needed to complete certain activity pages. These activities can also be completed on the free Chapter Review days that follow the completion of each chapter (optional special projects on page **313**).

- **Written Narration pages:** These pages are included for the older child who would like a place to write about his or her history chapter. Each chapter's question is on the back of the teacher pages and may be assigned at the end of the chapter.

- **Book of Service:** This book with information starting on page **263** is meant to be cut apart and assembled into a small book. Students record something they have done for someone else every week. Instructions are included, and the activity is optional.

- **Artist Study**: A quick introduction to an influential artist in history. Includes a variety of art activity ideas. The journal prompts can also be used as oral narration questions.

- **Learn the Presidents, Part 2:** This ongoing activity encourages students to memorize the last 23 presidents. They will have learned the first 22 presidents the previous year in Volume 2. This activity is optional and on page **319**.

- **My Timeline Manipulative**: A timeline is a way to organize events of history in a logical, chronological way. If you would like to make this timeline element a part of a student's lesson, take some time to look over the important events of the current chapter he or she is studying upon reaching the My Timeline section of this Teacher Guide. When creating their timeline, students can use the sketches provided in the back of this Teacher Guide. They may also choose to draw their own historical images or find them online. Use the timeline chart from the back and add information with each new lesson. It can be cut out and taped or glued together, and then hung on the wall. See the example from *America's Story 2* Teacher Guide below.

Adjust if needed! If the student is not yet ready to write answers to all questions or journaling prompts, simply have him or her give the answers orally. An alternative for a younger child would be to simply draw or color a picture showing his or her response to what he or she is learning. These pages can then be hole-punched and placed in the student's notebook.

Teaching Tips for Struggling Learners

✓ Look through this book and the student **textbook** and decide which material is the most important for your student to learn permanently. Before you even start the program with your student, write those chosen concepts on index cards. As you go through the course, use them to review.

✓ Connect all new information to something familiar. It is easier for any of us to permanently remember something when we have something familiar to tie it to. Teach your student mnemonic devices.

✓ Hands-on activities! Most children remember better the more senses they use. Just hearing it is not enough for most of us; we need to write about it, see it, and create it.

✓ Review often! Spend the entire week really getting into the story. Take time to plan crafts, skits, and anything else you can think of that will cement the story for your students. All children benefit from review. (Adults do too!) Ideas are included in the special projects section of this Teacher Guide.

✓ Encouragement — something so simple but so profound. Words of encouragement are always remembered.

✓ For most students who struggle, repetition is the key. The more times they hear it, the more likely they will be to remember it. Don't be afraid to re-read a chapter as a bedtime story. Or, if students can read on their own, let them re-read it. As they read, they can point out words they may not know.

✓ Show the students how the story relates to them. Talk about how they can apply it to themselves.

✓ Last, but most certainly NOT least, pray with your students. Teach them to pray for understanding and the ability to learn. Let them see you praying for them.

The Importance of Narration

Narration helps students to analyze a story and to choose the parts they deem important to them; it makes the thoughts their own, not someone else's.

How do you use narration as a learning tool?

After reading a chosen portion of a living book, have students retell in their own words what you just read. By having students retell or narrate, they are making the knowledge their own. It really is quite simple!

What if a student makes a mistake in the retelling of the storyline?

Years ago my son retold me a chapter from "Freedom Train," a story about the Underground Railroad. He was convinced that this was a train that ran underground much like a subway train.

When something like this happens, gently correct the misunderstood information without making the child feel bad. With my son, I have learned to tell him about when I have made silly mistakes. It helps him to understand that everyone does, and it is through these mistakes we learn our most lasting lessons.

Here are some sample narration prompts:

- ✔ And then what happened?
- ✔ Could you describe that in a little more detail?
- ✔ What did he do next?
- ✔ How did this make you feel?

Try to let your child think through the retelling by him or herself. Only use the prompts if absolutely necessary. Never, ever criticize a student's attempt at narrating. Be encouraging, and he or she will improve!

Forming a Relationship with Knowledge

Encouragement from me to you…

How many of us grew up with the "fill-in-the-blank" approach to education? I did. Fortunately I had a dad who did not grow up that way; he had experienced the living, breathing education of a one-room school house. My dad knew that a child's mind was much bigger than the "snacksize-baggie-brain" much of our current culture believes children to have.

How is it possible that a child, such as myself, who dutifully sat for hours a day filling in blanks, correcting the problems that the teacher key deemed "wrong!" could grow up to LOVE learning? Even though I did "my time at the desk," I give all credit of my real education to my dad. Those many, many times when he stopped walking to point at the brilliant night sky, teaching me the constellations or explaining the phenomenon of the Aurora Borealis, the historical fiction he would surprise me with even when money was nonexistent, the set of laminated maps and beautifully bound picture books of animals, the time spent just talking about who God really is, the always-accepting-of-me look ever present in his eyes…these are what made my true education.

All the blanks I filled, chopped-up bits of information I read, and sentences I diagrammed were all washed away within months. The relationship with real stories and life through my relationship with my dad never left me, and it is still the very foundation of who I am. Never underestimate your relationship with your children. It is a powerful tool that can be used to the glory of God in an astounding way.

Those of you who are new to teaching may be overwhelmed with the logistics of educating children. Please don't be. Pray for guidance. Accept life with all its imperfections. **<u>Choose</u>** love, joy, and peace. Lean not on your own understanding. Know that you are going to be learning more than your children. Keep growing; keep learning; lead by example. **<u>Know</u>** God knows and loves you and your children, and He has great plans for your lives.

First Semester Suggested Daily Schedule

Date	Day	Assignment	Due Date	✓	Grade
		First Semester–First Quarter			
Week 1	Day 1	Chapter 1: The Story of Teddy Roosevelt Read pages 5–7 • *America's Story 3* • (AS)			
	Day 2	Chapter 1: The Story of Teddy Roosevelt • Read pages 8–14 • (AS)			
	Day 3	Chapter 1: The Story of Teddy Roosevelt Complete activity pages 21–24 • Teacher Guide • (TG)			
	Day 4	Chapter 1: The Story of Teddy Roosevelt Complete activity pages 25–26 • (TG)			
	Day 5	Complete Chapter 1 timeline pages 27–28 • (TG)			
Week 2	Day 6	Chapter 1 Review Day: finish chapter materials or special projects if needed.			
	Day 7	Chapter 2: Presidents for Change • Read pages 15–17 • (AS)			
	Day 8	Chapter 2: Presidents for Change • Read pages 18–24 • (AS)			
	Day 9	Chapter 2: Presidents for Change Complete activity pages 29–32 • (TG)			
	Day 10	Chapter 2: Presidents for Change Complete activity pages 33–34 • (TG)			
Week 3	Day 11	Complete Chapter 2 timeline pages 35–36 • (TG)			
	Day 12	Chapter 2 Review Day: finish chapter materials or special projects if needed.			
	Day 13	Chapter 3: The Story of the Wright Brothers Read pages 25–27 • (AS)			
	Day 14	Chapter 3: The Story of the Wright Brothers Read pages 28–34 • (AS)			
	Day 15	Chapter 3: The Story of the Wright Brothers Complete activity pages 37–40 • (TG)			
Week 4	Day 16	Chapter 3: The Story of the Wright Brothers Complete activity pages 41–42 • (TG)			
	Day 17	Complete Chapter 3 timeline pages 43–44 • (TG)			
	Day 18	Chapter 3 Review Day: finish chapter materials or special projects if needed.			
	Day 19	Chapter 4: The Affordable Model Ts • Read pages 35–38 • (AS)			
	Day 20	Chapter 4: The Affordable Model Ts • Read pages 39–44 • (AS)			
Week 5	Day 21	Chapter 4: The Affordable Model Ts Complete activity pages 45–48 • (TG)			
	Day 22	Chapter 4: The Affordable Model Ts Complete activity pages 49–50 • (TG)			
	Day 23	Complete Chapter 4 timeline pages 51–52 • (TG)			
	Day 24	Chapter 4 Review Day: finish chapter materials or special projects if needed.			
	Day 25	Chapter 5: The Story of the Titanic • Read pages 45–47 • (AS)			

Date	Day	Assignment	Due Date	✓	Grade
Week 6	Day 26	Chapter 5: The Story of the Titanic • Read pages 48–54 • (AS)			
	Day 27	Chapter 5: The Story of the Titanic Complete activity pages 53–56 • (TG)			
	Day 28	Chapter 5: The Story of the Titanic Complete activity pages 57–58 • (TG)			
	Day 29	Complete Chapter 5 timeline pages 59–60 Read Artist Study page 61 • (TG) Complete activity of choice on page 62 • (TG)			
	Day 30	Chapter 5 Review Day: finish chapter materials or special projects if needed.			
Week 7	Day 31	Chapter 6: World Turmoil • Read pages 55–57 • (AS)			
	Day 32	Chapter 6: World Turmoil • Read pages 58–64 • (AS)			
	Day 33	Chapter 6: World Turmoil • Complete activity pages 63–68 • (TG)			
	Day 34	Chapter 6: World Turmoil • Complete activity pages 69–70 • (TG)			
	Day 35	Complete Chapter 6 timeline pages 71–72 • (TG)			
Week 8	Day 36	Chapter 6 Review Day: finish chapter materials or special projects if needed.			
	Day 37	Chapter 7: America After WWI • Read page 65 to the narration break on page 68 • (AS)			
	Day 38	Chapter 7: America After WWI • Read pages 68–74 • (AS)			
	Day 39	Chapter 7: America After WWI Complete activity pages 73–76 • (TG)			
	Day 40	Chapter 7: America After WWI Complete activity pages 77–78 • (TG)			
Week 9	Day 41	Complete Chapter 7 timeline pages 79–80 • (TG)			
	Day 42	Chapter 7 Review Day: finish chapter materials or special projects if needed.			
	Day 43	Review Day: review previous worksheets			
	Day 44	Complete **Review Sheet I** • Page 271 • (TG)			
	Day 45	Chapter 8: Crash! • Read pages 75–77 • (AS)			
First Semester-Second Quarter					
Week 1	Day 46	Chapter 8: Crash! • Read pages 78–84 • (AS)			
	Day 47	Chapter 8: Crash! • Complete activity pages 81–84 • (TG)			
	Day 48	Chapter 8: Crash! • Complete activity pages 85–86 • (TG)			
	Day 49	Complete Chapter 8 timeline pages 87–88 • (TG)			
	Day 50	Chapter 8 Review Day: finish chapter materials or special projects if needed.			
Week 2	Day 51	Chapter 9: The Great Depression • Read page 85 to the narration break on page 88 • (AS)			
	Day 52	Chapter 9: The Great Depression • Read pages 88–94 • (AS)			
	Day 53	Chapter 9: The Great Depression Complete activity pages 89–92 • (TG)			
	Day 54	Chapter 9: The Great Depression Complete activity pages 93–94 • (TG)			
	Day 55	Complete Chapter 9 timeline pages 95–96 • (TG)			

Date	Day	Assignment	Due Date	✓	Grade
Week 3	Day 56	Chapter 9 Review Day: finish chapter materials or special projects if needed.			
	Day 57	Chapter 10: The World at War • Read pages 95–97 • (AS)			
	Day 58	Chapter 10: The World at War • Read pages 98–104 • (AS)			
	Day 59	Chapter 10: The World at War Complete activity pages 97–102 • (TG)			
	Day 60	Chapter 10: The World at War Complete activity pages 103–104 • (TG)			
Week 4	Day 61	Complete Chapter 10 timeline pages 105–106 • (TG) Read Artist Study on page 107 • (TG) Complete activity of choice on page 108 • (TG)			
	Day 62	Chapter 10 Review Day: finish chapter materials or special projects if needed.			
	Day 63	Chapter 11: America at War, Part One • Read pages 105–107 • (AS)			
	Day 64	Chapter 11: America at War, Part One • Read pages 108–114 • (AS)			
	Day 65	Chapter 11: America at War, Part One Complete activity pages 109–112 • (TG)			
Week 5	Day 66	Chapter 11: America at War, Part One Complete activity pages 113–114 • (TG)			
	Day 67	Complete Chapter 11 timeline pages 115–116 • (TG)			
	Day 68	Chapter 11 Review Day: finish chapter materials or special projects if needed.			
	Day 69	Chapter 12: America at War, Part Two • Read pages 115–118 • (AS)			
	Day 70	Chapter 12: America at War, Part Two • Read pages 119–124 • (AS)			
Week 6	Day 71	Chapter 12: America at War, Part Two Complete activity pages 117–120 • (TG)			
	Day 72	Chapter 12: America at War, Part Two Complete activity pages 121–122 • (TG)			
	Day 73	Complete Chapter 12 timeline pages 123–124 • (TG)			
	Day 74	Chapter 12 Review Day: finish chapter materials or special projects if needed.			
	Day 75	Chapter 13: Life on the Homefront • Read page 125 to the narration break on page 128 • (AS)			
Week 7	Day 76	Chapter 13: Life on the Homefront • Read pages 128–134 • (AS)			
	Day 77	Chapter 13: Life on the Homefront Complete activity pages 125–128 • (TG)			
	Day 78	Chapter 13: Life on the Homefront Complete activity pages 129–132 • (TG)			
	Day 79	Complete Chapter 13 timeline pages 133–134 • (TG)			
	Day 80	Chapter 13 Review Day: finish chapter materials or special projects if needed.			

Date	Day	Assignment	Due Date	✓	Grade
Week 8	Day 81	Chapter 14: The Cold War • Read pages 135–137 • (AS)			
	Day 82	Chapter 14: The Cold War • Read pages 138–144 • (AS)			
	Day 83	Chapter 14: The Cold War Complete activity pages 135–138 • (TG)			
	Day 84	Chapter 14: The Cold War Complete activity pages 139–140 • (TG)			
	Day 85	Complete Chapter 14 timeline pages 141–142 • (TG)			
Week 9	Day 86	Chapter 14 Review Day: finish chapter materials or special projects if needed.			
	Day 87	Review Day: review previous worksheets			
	Day 88	Complete **Review Sheet II** • Pages 273–276 • (TG)			
	Day 89	Chapter 15: The Golden Age of America Read pages 145–147 • (AS)			
	Day 90	Chapter 15: The Golden Age of America Read pages 148–154 • (AS)			
		Mid-Term Grade			

Second Semester Suggested Daily Schedule

Date	Day	Assignment	Due Date	✓	Grade
		Second Semester-Third Quarter			
Week 1	Day 91	Chapter 15: The Golden Age of America Complete activity pages 143–146 • (TG)			
	Day 92	Chapter 15: The Golden Age of America Complete activity pages 147–148 • (TG)			
	Day 93	Complete Chapter 15 timeline pages 149–150 • (TG) Read Artist Study page 151 • (TG) Complete activity of choice on page 152 • (TG)			
	Day 94	Chapter 15 Review Day: finish chapter materials or special projects if needed.			
	Day 95	Chapter 16: Tumultuous Times • Read page 155 to the narration break on page 158 • (AS)			
Week 2	Day 96	Chapter 16: Tumultuous Times • Read pages 158–164 • (AS)			
	Day 97	Chapter 16: Tumultuous Times Complete activity pages 153–156 • (TG)			
	Day 98	Chapter 16: Tumultuous Times Complete activity pages 157–158 • (TG)			
	Day 99	Complete Chapter 16 timeline pages 159–160 • (TG)			
	Day 100	Chapter 16 Review Day: finish chapter materials or special projects if needed.			
Week 3	Day 101	Chapter 17: Changing Times • Read pages 165–167 • (AS)			
	Day 102	Chapter 17: Changing Times • Read pages 168–174 • (AS)			
	Day 103	Chapter 17: Changing Times Complete activity pages 161–164 • (TG)			
	Day 104	Chapter 17: Changing Times Complete activity pages 165–166 • (TG)			
	Day 105	Complete Chapter 17 timeline pages 167–168 • (TG)			
Week 4	Day 106	Chapter 17 Review Day: finish chapter materials or special projects if needed.			
	Day 107	Chapter 18: The Civil Rights Movement Read pages 175–177 • (AS)			
	Day 108	Chapter 18: The Civil Rights Movement Read pages 178–184 • (AS)			
	Day 109	Chapter 18: The Civil Rights Movement Complete activity pages 169–172 • (TG)			
	Day 110	Chapter 18: The Civil Rights Movement Complete activity pages 173–174 • (TG)			
Week 5	Day 111	Complete Chapter 18 timeline pages 175–176 • (TG)			
	Day 112	Chapter 18 Review Day: finish chapter materials or special projects if needed.			
	Day 113	Chapter 19: 1970s Politics and Fashion Read page 185 to the narration break on page 188 • (AS)			
	Day 114	Chapter 19: 1970s Politics and Fashion Read pages 188–194 • (AS)			
	Day 115	Chapter 19: 1970s Politics and Fashion Complete activity pages 177–180 • (TG)			

Date	Day	Assignment	Due Date	✓	Grade
Week 6	Day 116	Chapter 19: 1970s Politics and Fashion Complete activity pages 181–182 • (TG)			
	Day 117	Complete Chapter 19 timeline pages 183–184 • (TG)			
	Day 118	Chapter 19 Review Day: finish chapter materials or special projects if needed.			
	Day 119	Chapter 20: Political Scandals and Gasoline Shortages Read pages 195–197 • (AS)			
	Day 120	Chapter 20: Political Scandals and Gasoline Shortages Read pages 198–204 • (AS)			
Week 7	Day 121	Chapter 20: Political Scandals and Gasoline Shortages Complete activity pages 185–188 • (TG)			
	Day 122	Chapter 20: Political Scandals and Gasoline Shortages Complete activity pages 189–190 • (TG)			
	Day 123	Complete Chapter 20 timeline pages 191–192 • (TG) Read Artist Study page 193 • (TG) Complete activity of choice on page 194 • (TG)			
	Day 124	Chapter 20 Review Day: finish chapter materials or special projects if needed.			
	Day 125	Chapter 21: The 1980s, Part One • Read pages 205–207 • (AS)			
Week 8	Day 126	Chapter 21: The 1980s, Part One • Read pages 208–214 • (AS)			
	Day 127	Chapter 21: The 1980s, Part One Complete activity pages 195–198 • (TG)			
	Day 128	Chapter 21: The 1980s, Part One Complete activity pages 199–200 • (TG)			
	Day 129	Complete Chapter 21 timeline pages 201–202 • (TG)			
	Day 130	Chapter 21 Review Day: finish chapter materials or special projects if needed.			
Week 9	Day 131	Review Day: review previous worksheets			
	Day 132	Complete **Review Sheet III** • Pages 277–278 • (TG)			
	Day 133	Chapter 22: The 1980s, Part Two • Read pages 215–217 • (AS)			
	Day 134	Chapter 22: The 1980s, Part Two • Read pages 218–224 • (AS)			
	Day 135	Chapter 22: The 1980s, Part Two Complete activity pages 203–206 • (TG)			
Second Semester-Fourth Quarter					
Week 1	Day 136	Chapter 22: The 1980s, Part Two Complete activity pages 207–208 • (TG)			
	Day 137	Complete Chapter 22 timeline pages 209–210 • (TG)			
	Day 138	Chapter 22 Review Day: finish chapter materials or special projects if needed.			
	Day 139	Chapter 23: The 1990s, Part One • Read pages 225–227 • (AS)			
	Day 140	Chapter 23: The 1990s, Part One • Read pages 228–234 • (AS)			

Date	Day	Assignment	Due Date	✓	Grade
Week 2	Day 141	Chapter 23: The 1990s, Part One Complete activity pages 211–214 • (TG)			
	Day 142	Chapter 23: The 1990s, Part One Complete activity pages 215–216 • (TG)			
	Day 143	Complete Chapter 23 timeline pages 217–218 • (TG)			
	Day 144	Chapter 23 Review Day: finish chapter materials or special projects if needed.			
	Day 145	Chapter 24: The 1990s, Part Two • Read page 235 to the narration break on page 237 • (AS)			
Week 3	Day 146	Chapter 24: The 1990s, Part Two • Read pages 237–244 • (AS)			
	Day 147	Chapter 24: The 1990s, Part Two Complete activity pages 219–222 • (TG)			
	Day 148	Chapter 24: The 1990s, Part Two Complete activity pages 223–224 • (TG)			
	Day 149	Complete Chapter 24 timeline pages 225–226 • (TG)			
	Day 150	Chapter 24 Review Day: finish chapter materials or special projects if needed.			
Week 4	Day 151	Chapter 25: The Strange Election of 2000 Read pages 245–247 • (AS)			
	Day 152	Chapter 25: The Strange Election of 2000 Read pages 248–254 • (AS)			
	Day 153	Chapter 25: The Strange Election of 2000 Complete activity pages 227–230 • (TG)			
	Day 154	Chapter 25: The Strange Election of 2000 Complete activity pages 231–232 • (TG)			
	Day 155	Complete Chapter 25 timeline pages 233–234 • (TG) Read Artist Study page 235 • (TG) Complete activity of choice on page 236 • (TG)			
Week 5	Day 156	Chapter 25 Review Day: finish chapter materials or special projects if needed.			
	Day 157	Chapter 26: "Evil, Despicable Acts of Terror" Read pages 255–257 • (AS)			
	Day 158	Chapter 26: "Evil, Despicable Acts of Terror" Read pages 258–264 • (AS)			
	Day 159	Chapter 26: "Evil, Despicable Acts of Terror" Complete activity pages 237–240 • (TG)			
	Day 160	Chapter 26: "Evil, Despicable Acts of Terror" Complete activity pages 241–242 • (TG)			
Week 6	Day 161	Complete Chapter 26 timeline pages 243–244 • (TG)			
	Day 162	Chapter 26 Review Day: finish chapter materials or special projects if needed.			
	Day 163	Chapter 27: More Recent History • Read page 265 to the narration break on page 267 • (AS)			
	Day 164	Chapter 27: More Recent History • Read pages 267–274 • (AS)			
	Day 165	Chapter 27: More Recent History Complete activity pages 245–248 • (TG)			

Date	Day	Assignment	Due Date	✓	Grade
Week 7	Day 166	Chapter 27: More Recent History Complete activity pages 249–250 • (TG)			
	Day 167	Complete Chapter 27 timeline pages 251–252 • (TG)			
	Day 168	Chapter 27 Review Day: finish chapter materials or special projects if needed.			
	Day 169	Chapter 28: Protectors of Our Freedom Read pages 275–277 • (AS)			
	Day 170	Chapter 28: Protectors of Our Freedom Read pages 278–284 • (AS)			
Week 8	Day 171	Chapter 28: Protectors of Our Freedom Complete activity pages 253–256 • (TG)			
	Day 172	Chapter 28: Protectors of Our Freedom Complete activity pages 257–258 • (TG)			
	Day 173	Complete Chapter 28 timeline pages 259–260 • (TG) Read Artist Study page 261 • (TG) Complete activity of choice on page 262 • (TG)			
	Day 174	Chapter 28 Review Day: finish chapter materials or special projects if needed.			
	Day 175	Review Day: review previous worksheets			
Week 9	Day 176	Complete **Review Sheet IV** • Pages 279–280 • (TG)			
	Day 177	Review worksheets from Chapters 1–28.			
	Day 178	Review Review Sheets I–IV.			
	Day 179	Complete **Final Review Sheet, Part I** • Pages 281–282 • (TG)			
	Day 180	Complete **Final Review Sheet, Part II** • Pages 283–284 • (TG)			
		Final Grade			

World Map

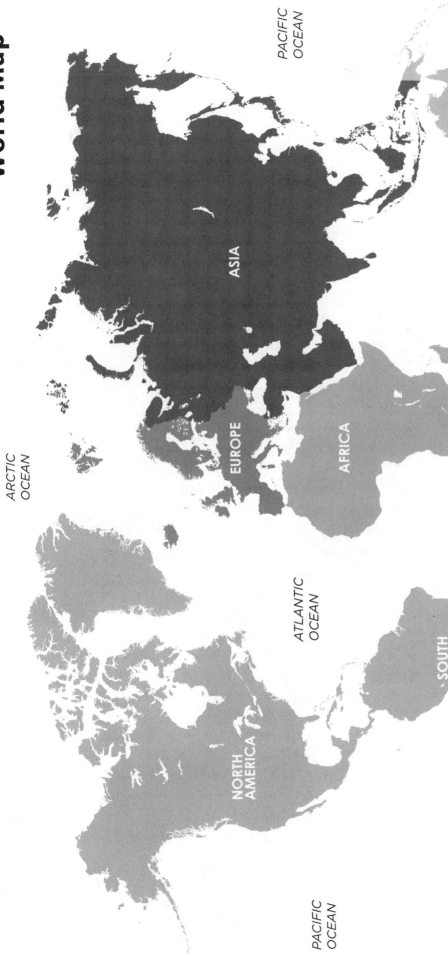

PACIFIC
OCEAN

ASIA

ARCTIC
OCEAN

EUROPE

AFRICA

AUSTRALIA

ANTARCTICA

NORTH
AMERICA

ATLANTIC
OCEAN

SOUTH
AMERICA

PACIFIC
OCEAN

United States Map

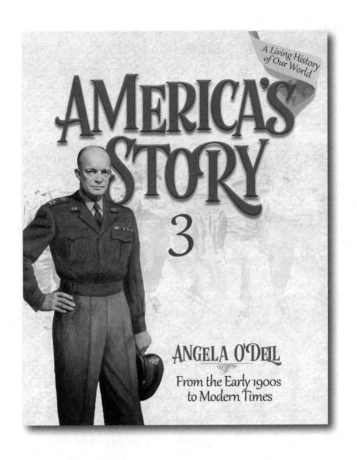

Chapter Activity Pages

for Use with

America's Story 3

 **MAP ADVENTURES** Name _____

The Story of Teddy Roosevelt. Review the map on pages 10–11 of your student book, which shows the lands in the United States under federal control, and answer the following questions. Note that on a map, north is the top, south is the bottom, east is to the right, and west is to the left.

1. Which part of the country has the most federally-controlled lands — eastern, midwest, or western America?_____

2. Which two states have the most area controlled by the Bureau of Land Management?

   _____

3. Which government agency controls the biggest area of land in Oklahoma?

   _____

4. Which government agency has control of the largest amount of land across the United States and not just in the western states? _____ (Hint! Which color is shown most across the whole map?)

5. Which government agency controls the biggest area of land across the middle of Alaska?

   _____

Draw it!

In this box, draw the outline of the state that you live in. Put a large star where you live within the state. Then color the areas of the state that are under federal control as shown on the map in your student book on pages 10–11.

My State

Word Collectors:

6. Did you find the chapter's special word? Write it below:

_____

Now, collect three other words you learned from this chapter by writing them below!

7. _____ 8. _____ 9. _____

Narrate or write the meaning of the words you have found:

10. _____

_____

11. _____

_____

12. _____

_____

Unscramble!

Can you figure out some of the jobs that Teddy had in his lifetime? Unscramble the following words:

13. dsiterPen: _____

14. misCocsilenroemiPo: _____ _____

15. htourA: _____

16. phiytefeuSfDr: _____ _____

17. bnlsAsmemya: _____

The Story of Teddy Roosevelt. Pretend you've just been hired to work for one of the government agencies mentioned on page 11. Select the one you prefer, then write a letter to your local newspaper explaining to them what your new job consists of and why the job is needed.

_____

_____

_____

_____

_____

_____

_____

_____

_____

_____

_____

_____

_____

_____

_____

_____

_____

_____

_____

_____

_____

My Timeline Manipulative. A timeline is a way to organize events of history in a logical, chronological way. If you would like to make this timeline element a part of a student's lesson, take some time to look over the important events of the current chapter. When creating their timeline, students can use sketches provided in the back of this Teacher Guide on pages 335–341. They may also choose to draw their own historical images or find them online. Use the timeline chart from the back and add information with each new lesson.

2 PRESIDENTS FOR CHANGE

Materials needed for this chapter:

✔ Student Activity Pages

✔ Pencil/eraser

✔ Colored pencils or crayons

✔ Globe or atlas

✔ Optional: Books or websites about the presidents of this time period

Oral Narration Questions and Answers

Q. Retell what we have read so far about the Progressive Movement.

A. Allow your student to tell freely his or her favorite part — but the student needs to include information (or ideas) about government being needed to solve issues and create laws that provided safe food and other things. After doing so, discuss any details that you feel are important for him or her to understand and remember.

Q. Retell and discuss what we have read today about Presidents Taft and Wilson.

A. Again, allow your student to tell what stood out to him or her from today's reading. Discuss any details you feel are important for him or her to understand and remember.

Optional Digging Deeper

✔ **Famous homeschoolers:** Woodrow Wilson, who struggled with what was probably dyslexia, or a similar learning difference, was only one famous homeschooler! Your student may enjoy discovering other major historical figures who were also homeschooled.

Written Narration Idea for Older Students:

What do you think are the pros and cons of a government set up with Progressive ideals?

_____

_____

_____

_____

_____

_____

_____

_____

MAP ADVENTURES

Name _____

Presidents for Change. Wow! You get to be part of the design of the Panama Canal. Look at this map — and using three different marker colors, draw three possible routes for the canal.

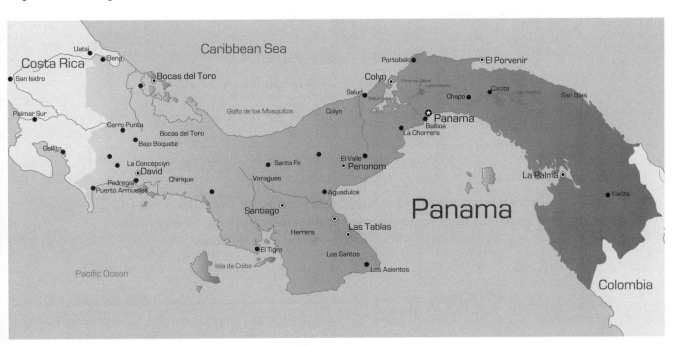

1. Why was the Panama Canal built?

_____

_____

_____

2. What was the Progressive Era in America?

_____

_____

_____

Copywork:

> **Do what you can, with what you have, where you are.**
> **—Teddy Roosevelt**

_____

_____

> **Politics make me sick.**
> **—William Howard Taft**

_____

_____

> **America was established not to create wealth but to realize a vision,**
> **to realize an ideal — to discover and maintain liberty among men.**
> **—Woodrow Wilson**

_____

_____

_____

A Promise!

The following is the presidential oath of office:

> I do solemnly swear (or affirm) that I will faithfully execute the Office of President of the United States, and will to the best of my Ability, preserve, protect and defend the Constitution of the United States.

3. From the wording of this oath, what do you think is the primary job of the president?

_____

_____

_____

_____

SKETCHING

Name _____

Presidents for Change. These three men (Roosevelt, Taft, and Wilson) would face one another in the presidential election of 1912. Choose one of these three presidents and create an election poster in support of your candidate. Be sure to list his party and give a reason for someone to vote for your candidate.

1. Why was Woodrow Wilson homeschooled?

_____

_____

_____

2. How did the split in the Republican Party between President Taft and former president Teddy Roosevelt help President Woodrow Wilson win the election?

_____

_____

_____

Who Did What?

Fill in the blank with the name of which president (Roosevelt, Taft, Wilson) did the following:

3. Created the "Bull Moose" Party. _____

4. Focused on reforming the civil service and ending monopolies. _____

5. Earned a Ph.D. in history and political science. _____

6. Was the nation's 26th president. _____

7. First civilian governor of the newly annexed Philippines. _____

8. His election slogan was "He kept us out of war." _____

Word Collectors:

9. Did you find the chapter's special word? Write it below:

_____

Now, collect three other words you learned from this chapter by writing them below!

10. _____   11. _____   12. _____

Make sure you can explain the words to your teacher.

Presidents for Change. Pretend you are helping build the Panama Canal. It's tough work!
Write a letter to a relative or friend explaining what a typical day is like working on the canal.

_____

_____

_____

_____

_____

_____

_____

_____

_____

_____

_____

_____

_____

_____

_____

_____

_____

_____

_____

_____

My Timeline Manipulative. A timeline is a way to organize events of history in a logical, chronological way. If you would like to make this timeline element a part of a student's lesson, take some time to look over the important events of the current chapter. When creating their timeline, students can use sketches provided in the back of this Teacher Guide on pages 335–341. They may also choose to draw their own historical images or find them online. Use the timeline chart from the back and add information with each new lesson.

3 THE STORY OF THE WRIGHT BROTHERS

Materials needed for this chapter:

- ✔ Student Activity Pages
- ✔ Pencil/eraser
- ✔ Colored pencils or crayons
- ✔ Globe or atlas
- ✔ Optional: Books or websites about the the early flying machines

Oral Narration Questions and Answers

Q. Talk about how God's design of bird wings influenced the Wright brothers.

A. Be sure the student includes the reaction of other people to the Wright brothers' ideas.

Q. Tell your favorite part of the Wright brothers' story.

A. Allow your student to tell you what stood out to him or her from the chapter. Ask tyour student why he or she thinks the Wright brothers managed to succeed while others failed.

Optional Digging Deeper

- ✔ Who else was trying to engineer wings for man at this time? Let your student discover some of the other flying machine inventions of this time period.

Written Narration Idea for Older Students:

What did you learn about the Wright brothers that shows you they loved to experiment and solve problems? What would it have been like for them to help develop and see the many advances in flight over the years?

_____

_____

_____

_____

_____

_____

_____

_____

SKETCHING

Name _____

The Story of the Wright Brothers. Draw your own "flying machine"! Be creative and color in your newly designed invention when you are done!

1. What first sparked the Wright brothers' interest in flight?

_____

_____

_____

2. What were some of the things that the Wright brothers invented or designed?

_____

_____

_____

3. What did they use the money for that they earned from repairing and selling bicycles?

_____

_____

_____

4. Imagine you are Wilbur or Orville Wright. Write a diary entry following the historic three-second
    flight of December 14, 1903, sharing your thoughts and dreams.

_____

_____

_____

_____

_____

_____

_____

_____

_____

_____

_____

_____

_____

_____

MAP ADVENTURES

Name _____

The Story of the Wright Brothers. Page 30 in your student book includes two maps — choose one to recreate below:

In the News!

1. There were some very strange-looking flying machines as people tried to create inventions that would fly. Imagine you went to a special air show where these inventions were being demonstrated. In the space below, write a short news article describing a few of the inventions you see on pages 32–33 in your student book.

_____

_____

_____

_____

_____

_____

_____

_____

Word Collectors:

2. Did you find the chapter's special word? Write it below:

   _____

Now, collect three other words you learned from this chapter by writing them below!

3. _____   4. _____   5. _____

Make sure you can explain the words to your teacher.

The Story of the Wright Brothers. Pretend you are a newspaper reporter assigned to cover Charles Lindbergh's flight across the Atlantic Ocean. You are sent to Paris so that you can be there when he lands. What was that moment like? Did you get a chance to interview Lindbergh? Write a newspaper article describing what happened.

_____

_____

_____

_____

_____

_____

_____

_____

_____

_____

_____

_____

_____

_____

_____

_____

_____

_____

My Timeline Manipulative. A timeline is a way to organize events of history in a logical, chronological way. If you would like to make this timeline element a part of a student's lesson, take some time to look over the important events of the current chapter. When creating their timeline, students can use sketches provided in the back of this Teacher Guide on pages 335–341. They may also choose to draw their own historical images or find them online. Use the timeline chart from the back and add information with each new lesson.

THE AFFORDABLE MODEL TS

4

Dear Parent or Teacher,

There are some early films on the automobile at the Library of Congress archives (www. loc.gov)." There are also several very informative videos about Henry Ford and his industrialization of the automobile, available on YouTube™. Please do not allow your student to search for videos on the site; it is important that you find and prescreen any video that you want him or her to see beforehand. This site, like many others online, has content that is not appropriate for children, and these can appear in search results or in ads.

Google Books is also a wonderful resource for old books, industry materials, magazine files on Model Ts and other early vehicles as well that can be downloaded for free. These include one of the *Ford Times* — an early owner's magazine from the Ford Motor Company.

Materials needed for this chapter:

- ✔ Student Activity Pages
- ✔ Pencil/eraser
- ✔ Colored pencils or crayons
- ✔ Globe or atlas
- ✔ Optional: Books or websites about early automobiles. If you can find it, I recommend *Alice Ramsey's Grand Adventure* by Don Brown. This beautifully illustrated storybook tells of a fantastic cross-country road trip — the first one in history to be completed by a woman — in an automobile! The year is 1909. Worth searching for!

Oral Narration Questions and Answers

Q. Tell what you learned today about Henry Ford.

A. Allow your student to retell what he or she learned today. Discuss how much cars cost back then compared to cars today. (This may be a good time to talk about how a dollar was "worth more" during that time period compared to now.)

Q. Tell what your favorite part of the Model T "drive" was.

A. Make sure the student can articulate some details either about the amazingly sturdy and rugged Model T car or the way it performed while driving.

Optional Digging Deeper

- ✔ Who else was building cars at this time? How many different brands of American cars can you find?

Written Narration Idea for Older Students:

Henry Ford started the Detroit Automobile Company, which did not last. Describe why below.

SKETCHING

Name _____

The Affordable Model Ts. Henry Ford had a number of different patents. These include the different parts of the Model T and other vehicles or inventions. Draw your own Model T!

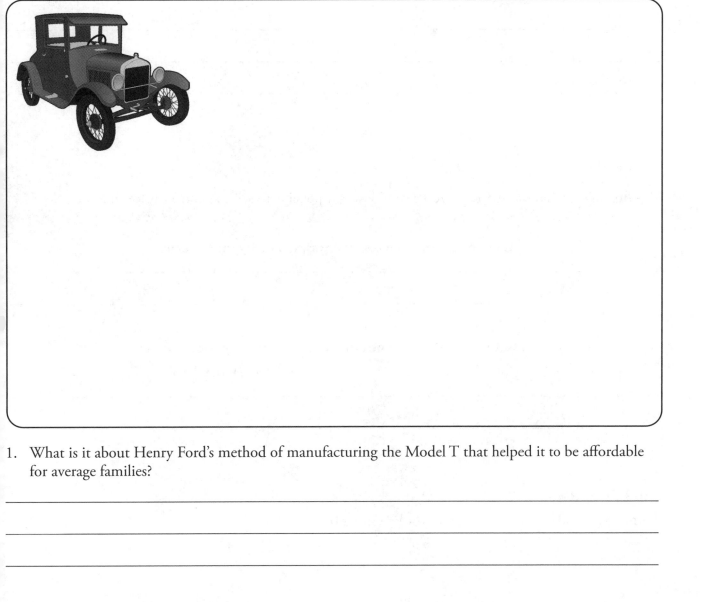

1. What is it about Henry Ford's method of manufacturing the Model T that helped it to be affordable for average families?

_____

_____

_____

2. Why was the assembly line so useful?

_____

_____

_____

Model T Salesman!

3. Imagine being a car salesman at a place that sells Model Ts. What would you say to encourage a family to purchase the automobile? You can either narrate your "sales pitch" or write it below. Be sure to include three positive aspects of the Model T in the sales pitch!

_____

_____

_____

_____

_____

Copywork:

This first one is from the article "Ford Prices: How is it possible to sell so good a car for so low a price."
—*Ford Times, Vol. 2*, 1908.

It's demand that makes business. Quantity makes price.

_____

_____

A business that makes nothing but money is a poor business.
—Henry Ford

_____

_____

Word Collectors:

4. Did you find the chapter's special word? Write it below:

_____

Now, collect three other words you learned from this chapter by writing them below!

5. _____   6. _____   7. _____

Use each word in a separate sentence for your teacher.

MAP ADVENTURES

Name _____

The Affordable Model Ts. The map for this chapter in your student book shows you how the popularity of automobiles like the Model T helped the creation and expansion of the road system across America. Now you get to be in charge of Chicago's street system. As you can see in this small portion of a bird's-eye view of the business district, there are street cars already operating in parts of the roads. Now you need to decide where you would put street signs to control traffic and prevent accidents between street cars and the new automobiles. Be sure to include at least one parking lot, so that people with their new Model Ts can drive them to work.

1. Mark the parking area with a green marker.

2. Mark the placement of street signs with the following:

   a. Blue for "slow" signs.

   b. Red for "Stop" signs.

   c. Purple for "one-way" signs. (This means traffic can only go one way on the street.)

3. How did the Model T change the world forever?

_____

_____

_____

Early automobiles did not have turn signals on them. Drivers had to develop hand signals so that other drivers would know which way they were going or when they were going to stop. Practice the following signals for right turn, left turn, and slow/stop that are still used in cycling today.

Left   **Right**   **Slow/Stop**

4. **Imagine!** Here is an image of your first car. Write a diary entry of your plans for a family trip to somewhere special.

_____

_____

_____

_____

_____

_____

_____

_____

_____

My Timeline!

The Affordable Model Ts. Pretend that you are working on the Ford assembly line making Model Ts. What is your job? What is your job like? Write a letter to a relative or friend explaining your work.

_____

_____

_____

_____

_____

_____

_____

_____

_____

_____

_____

_____

_____

_____

_____

_____

_____

_____

_____

_____

_____

My Timeline Manipulative. A timeline is a way to organize events of history in a logical, chronological way. If you would like to make this timeline element a part of a student's lesson, take some time to look over the important events of the current chapter. When creating their timeline, students can use sketches provided in the back of this Teacher Guide on pages 335–341. They may also choose to draw their own historical images or find them online. Use the timeline chart from the back and add information with each new lesson.

THE STORY OF THE TITANIC

5

Dear Parent or Teacher,

The *Titanic* disaster is a fascinating aspect of history. However, it is also the story of the tragic death of many people and whole families. While we do not dwell on a lot of specifics on these deaths, they are part of the history. Use your own discretion in allowing students to research or explore this history in the form of videos or books.

Materials needed for this chapter:

- ✔ Student Activity Pages
- ✔ Pencil/eraser
- ✔ Colored pencils or crayons
- ✔ Globe or atlas
- ✔ Optional: Books or websites about the sinking of the *Titanic*

Oral Narration Questions and Answers

Q. Tell what happened to the *Titanic*.

A. See what points your student found most interesting about the text and encourage him or her to share his or her thoughts.

Q. Retell Elizabeth Shute's story about the *Titanic*

A. Allow your student to share what details he or she can remember about this personal account.

Optional Digging Deeper

- ✔ **For older students only:** There are a number of documentaries about the *Titanic* that focus on a variety of topics regarding the sinking. It is always important to prescreen these to make sure the subject matter is appropriate for the age and sensitivities of your student.

Written Narration Idea for Older Students:

There were many people who traveled in steerage on the *Titanic*. Summarize the thoughts of Elizabeth Shute's story.

_____

_____

_____

_____

_____

_____

_____

_____

SKETCHING

Name _____

The Story of the _Titanic_. Draw an image of the _Titanic_ sailing the ocean before hitting the iceberg.

1. A person's experiences on the _Titanic_ were different depending on the class status you were as a passenger (first class, second class, or third class). If you could have bought a ticket to sail on the _Titanic_, which class of ticket would you have chosen? Why?

_____

_____

_____

2. Why was the ship thought to be "unsinkable"?

_____

_____

_____

_____

MAP ADVENTURES

Name _____

The Story of the _Titanic_. The _Titanic_ sank and was lost in the very deep waters of the North Atlantic Ocean. We know the coordinates (or location) of where the ship sank. You can use the numbers of the coordinates — representing longitude and latitude lines — to mark the location of the sinking on the map below.

The location of the ship is 12,600 feet down at 41.726931° N and 49.948253° W. The numbers are very detailed because finding a ship in a large area like the Atlantic Ocean means you have to be precise.

Let's simplify the numbers to make it easier for you to find and mark the location on the map: **Latitude 41.73° N and Longitude 49.95° W.**

Longitude are the lines that go north and south on the map. **Latitude** are the lines that go east and west on the map.

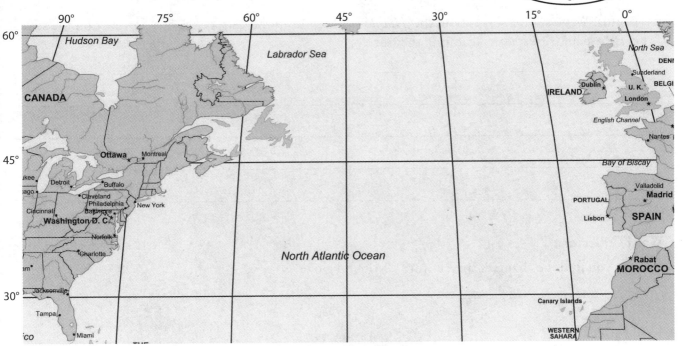

1. Why do you think that the story of the _Titanic_ is so unforgettable?

_____

_____

_____

_____

2. Why was it so important to future ship travelers that this tragedy be part of a U.S. Senate investigation?

_____

_____

_____

3. Imagine you are a reporter who has to do a story about the wreck of the *Titanic*. The headline of an article is the text that is written in large and bold text at the top to catch the attention of readers. What would the headline of your article be?

_____

_____

_____

4. **Bonus!** Write a short story about the *Titanic's* sinking from the perspective of a newsboy on the street corner selling newspapers featuring the story.

_____

_____

_____

_____

_____

Word Collectors:

5. Did you find the chapter's special word? Write it below:

_____

Now, collect three other words you learned from this chapter by writing them below!

6. _____   7. _____   8. _____

Be sure to explain the meaning of the words to your teacher. If you are confused about the meaning, see if you can figure it out by re-reading the sentence where it is found.

MY TIMELINE!

Name _____

The Story of the *Titanic*. Pretend that you are on the *Titanic*. You can be a crewmember, a first-class passenger, a second-class passenger, or a third-class passenger. The public is eager to hear your experiences. Write your own account of the sinking and how you managed to survive.

_____

_____

_____

_____

_____

_____

_____

_____

_____

_____

_____

_____

_____

_____

_____

_____

_____

_____

_____

_____

_____

My Timeline Manipulative. A timeline is a way to organize events of history in a logical, chronological way. If you would like to make this timeline element a part of a student's lesson, take some time to look over the important events of the current chapter. When creating their timeline, students can use sketches provided in the back of this Teacher Guide on pages 335–341. They may also choose to draw their own historical images or find them online. Use the timeline chart from the back and add information with each new lesson.

ARTIST STUDY

Name _____

Winsor McCay (Animator/Cartoonist). Winsor McCay is one of the most influential animators in American history, but many people have never even heard of him. Raised in Michigan, though he was likely born in Canada, McCay was a talented artist as a child. His family had wanted him to be a clerk and work in business, but he was more interested in drawing. He worked for years as a printer, sign painter, and artist for local newspapers. He also worked sketching people at dime museums. He was always popular with audiences because of how easily he could create realistic drawings of people in the crowd.

(1911, PD-US)

In 1903, he moved to New York City to become a cartoonist. He drew a number of popular comic strips. His most popular was about a boy named Nemo and his adventures in his dreams. Another popular comic strip focused on Little Sammy, who had an unfortunate habit of sneezing uncontrollably! Despite his popularity as a cartoonist, McCay also continued to entertain people at vaudeville shows with a drawing routine. Vaudeville was a form of entertainment popular in the early 20th century. Vaudeville shows featured a range of acts, including singers, musicians, and comedians. McCay liked to mix comedy into his drawing act.

He soon became interested in drawing animation. At this time, movies were still new. Others had done animation before, but their work had been simplistic. McCay's animation work, however, was sophisticated and pioneered techniques used decades later. Some of his more famous animation work included *Gertie the Dinosaur* and a depiction of the *Lusitania* sinking.

McCay ended up working for one of the most famous newspaper publishers at the time, William Randolph Hearst. However, Hearst didn't like McCay spending his free time animating, so he forbade him from doing his vaudeville work and drawing the animations and cartoons he really liked to do.

Example of Drawings by Winsor McCay

More Art by Winsor McCay

Choose one of the following activities to understand more about Winsor McCay's work.

1. You can either journal about or answer one or more of the following questions.

    ✔ In what ways are drawing a cartoon and animating different, and in what ways are they similar?

    ✔ How do you think McCay's vaudeville work influenced his career as an artist?

    ✔ Do you think of animation as art? Why or why not?

2. Do an art assessment.

    ✔ What do you notice about McCay's drawings when you first look at them?

    ✔ Do you think his animation work looks different from his cartoons? Why or why not?

    ✔ Do you think his drawings look modern? Why or why not?

3. Try it!

    ✔ You'll need a stack of lightweight paper and a pencil and something to color with (crayons, markers, colored pencils, etc.) for this activity.

    ✔ On the bottom page, near the bottom right corner, draw something. It could be someone getting ready to go for a run, or a getting ready to jump up and down, or getting ready to throw a ball.

    ✔ On each sheet of paper, draw whatever you are drawing continuing that action. Make sure the sequence makes sense. Someone wouldn't let go of the ball before they moved their arm backwards to throw, for example.

    ✔ Once you have finished, color your drawings.

    ✔ Now, hold your flipbook open and flip through the pages to watch your animation!

6 WORLD TURMOIL

Dear Parent or Teacher,

As with a study of any war, events that occurred during WWI can be disturbing. There are historical films and books written about the experiences of soldiers during the war, but these materials need to be carefully assessed to make sure they are appropriate for your student before you use them.

Materials needed for this chapter:

- ✔ Student Activity Pages
- ✔ Pencil/eraser
- ✔ Colored pencils or crayons
- ✔ Index cards
- ✔ Globe or atlas
- ✔ Optional: Books or websites about America's involvement in World War I

Oral Narration Questions and Answers

Q. Tell what you learned about World War I.

A. Make sure your student can articulate why America wanted to stay out of the war and how America finally got involved.

Q. Retell what we have learned today about the homefront during WWI.

A. Take the time to discuss the events and issues covered in this part of the chapter. Take extra time to talk about what the food shortage would have been like to children your student's age.

Optional Digging Deeper

- ✔ Your student may enjoy finding images of WWI propaganda posters. Talk to your student about the use of these posters. (They are carefully designed to stir up emotion — anger, fear, or even patriotism. Really effective posters stirred up as many emotions as possible!)

Written Narration Idea for Older Students:

What is trench foot?

_____

_____

_____

_____

_____

_____

_____

_____

LEARN ONE SOLDIER'S STORY

Some American soldiers wrote in diaries during their time overseas in World War I. Albert John Carpenter was just 19 when he enlisted along with other soldiers from the Texas and Oklahoma National Guard. He was lucky that he was only part of the fighting for a month, but as he titled his diary, it was "The Most Eventful Month of My Life." (Please note — the diary entries are presented with their original spelling.)

Friday 11 – 142nd casualtys still enlarging. Am very weak with only two good meals since on front. 12 a.m. a gas shell came over. Did not get my gas mask on quick enough. Sent to field hospital. Taken about 20 pills and sent back to the lines at 10 p.m.

Saturday 12 – My lungs are very soar and throughing up blood. Took charge of telephone at 2 p.m. on duty till 12 p.m. 144th Infantry goes over the top. Drives [the Germans] back. First hot meal since on front.

Sunday 13 – It has rained all day. [Germans] retreated 25 kilometers. Still sick from gas. Marched from St. Etienne to Vaux Champagne. Very, very tired.

Tuesday 15 – Rest all day. Thank God. [Germans] seem to be resting easy also. Nothing but artillery fire.

Wednesday 16 – Received letter from Mother.

Monday 21 – Still raining. Our holes get very much mudy and cold. On a detail to dig a dugout for Col. N. French layed down an artillery barrage which made smoke for miles, but still unable to advance.

Thursday 24 – Am now on front line with a telephone and a buzzer. Getting ready to go over the top. 142nd still losing in strength.

Friday 25 – Our eats have run out, but still trying to keep up good spirits. Have my phone in a shallow hole behind a rock wall. [Germans] throwing 88's and machine gun shells on us.

Saturday 26 – Preparing for the last battle. Many French and American artillery batteries set for action. About 40 machine guns several French mortars. No sleep, no eats, tired, blue and very homesick.

Albert J. Carpenter

War: World War I, 1914–1918

Branch: Army

Unit: Headquarters Company, 142nd Infantry Regiment, 36th Infantry Division

Service Location: Camp Bowie, Texas; Fort Sill, Oklahoma; France

Rank: Private

Albert Carpenter was known as "Bert" and carried a small New Testament with him. He had written the Morse Code alphabet on the inside cover. This picture is a postcard that Albert sent home to his mother. He wrote, "Dear Mother, here is a picture of the squad I was in. This is a frightful day. I do wish they would move us out of this place. I sign the pay roll in the morning and will be paid in about two weeks. Albert"

Information from the Library of Congress.

These are Albert Carpenter's military records — one is where he enlisted into the U.S. Army; the other is his honorable discharge from the service at the end of the war.

You can learn a lot about someone from records like these. Albert was given immunizations and received a special medal — the victory medal (shown below) — for his service. He was a student before joining the army. We know he did not serve on horseback, he enlisted in Oklahoma, and hadn't qualified as a marksman — someone who shoots very accurately. We know what battles he took part in and even his character — noted as excellent. You can even see a sample of Albert's handwriting at the bottom where he signed the enlistment document.

His discharge papers not only tell us when he left the service, they also tell us a physical description, where he was born, and at what military site from which he was discharged.

Genealogy is the study of family history — and you can find military records like these, as well as census reports and other information, from various public sources if you want to learn more about history and veterans within your own family. Some records go back before the Revolutionary War and even further if your ancestors came to America from countries like the United Kingdom, etc.

SKETCHING

Name _____

World Turmoil. It was very important that Americans save on food and other necessities as part of the war effort! Design and sketch a poster on cardstock or other paper to encourage people to not waste food.

Make a Menu! Plan a week's worth of meals using Hoover's Food Administration guidelines of:

1. Wheatless Monday:

_____

_____

2. Meatless Tuesday:

_____

_____

3. Wheatless Wednesday:

_____

_____

4. Porkless Thursday:

_____

_____

5. Regular Meal Friday:

_____

_____

6. Porkless Saturday:

_____

_____

Word Collectors:

7. Did you find the chapter's special word? Write it below:

_____

Now, collect three other words you learned from this chapter by writing them below!

8. _____ 9. _____ 10. _____

Make sure you can explain the meaning of the words to your teacher. If you are confused about the meaning, see if you can figure it out by re-reading the sentence where it is found or look it up in a dictionary.

11. Why did America finally have to join the conflicts of WWI?

_____

_____

_____

12. Having read Albert John Carpenter's diary, what do you think life was like for American soldiers in the trenches of WWI?

_____

_____

_____

Day 34

MAP ADVENTURES

Name _____

World Turmoil. Fill in this map with the names of the following countries: Soviet Union, Italy, Spain, Poland, Germany, France, and the United Kingdom.

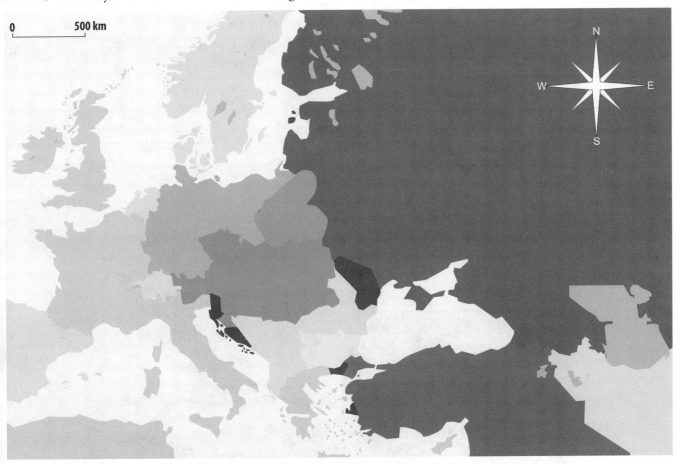

1. What was the nickname given to American troops in WWI? _____

2. What was the name of the ship that carried Americans that German U-boats sank during the war?

_____

3. What were some of the nicknames given to WWI?

_____

_____

_____

4. Describe what it was like to be an African American serving in WWI.

_____

_____

_____

5. How did WWI change job opportunities for women at this time?

_____

_____

_____

6. Why was it so easy for the Spanish flu to spread during WWI both in America and around the world?

_____

_____

_____

7. This image depicts the attack by German U-boat U-21 as passengers flee the sinking ship. Give a short report based on what you can see either from the perspective of a sailor of the U-boat or a passenger on the ship.

_____

_____

_____

_____

_____

_____

_____

MY TIMELINE!

Name _____

World Turmoil. Pretend that you are living during World War I. You can be a soldier or someone on the homefront. Write a diary entry describing what your day was like.

_____

_____

_____

_____

_____

_____

_____

_____

_____

_____

_____

_____

_____

_____

_____

_____

_____

_____

_____

_____

_____

_____

My Timeline Manipulative. A timeline is a way to organize events of history in a logical, chronological way. If you would like to make this timeline element a part of a student's lesson, take some time to look over the important events of the current chapter. When creating their timeline, students can use sketches provided in the back of this Teacher Guide on pages 335–341. They may also choose to draw their own historical images or find them online. Use the timeline chart from the back and add information with each new lesson.

AMERICA AFTER WWI

Materials needed for this chapter:

- ✓ Student Activity Pages
- ✓ Pencil/eraser
- ✓ Colored pencils or crayons
- ✓ Globe and/or atlas
- ✓ Optional: Books or websites about the 1920s or the Scopes Monkey Trial, such as *Scopes: Creation on Trial* (Master Books)

Oral Narration Questions and Answers

Q. Describe America after WWI.

A. Allow your student to retell what he or she learned today. Encourage him or her to elaborate on the details that show a contrast before and after the war.

Q. Talk about some of the problems America faced.

A. Allow your student to tell you what stood out to him or her from the chapter. Ask questions, if needed, to help your student give some specifics in his or her answer.

Optional Digging Deeper

- ✓ Your student may enjoy listening to a recording of Louis Armstrong singing "What a Wonderful World."

Written Narration Idea for Older Students:

What was Prohibition? Why didn't it work?

_____

_____

_____

_____

_____

_____

_____

_____

SKETCHING

Name _____

America After WWI. Batter up! Baseball became very popular at this time. So did baseball cards. Imagine you are part of a famous baseball team at the time. Create a name for your team and draw a baseball card featuring yourself!

1. How were people able to buy the conveniences they wanted at this time?

   _____

   _____

   _____

2. What were some of the ways that Americans had fun at this time?

   _____

   _____

   _____

3. While segregation and racism were still common, what African American music became part of popular culture?

   _____

   _____

   _____

4. How did women's fashions change during this time?

_____

_____

_____

_____

_____

_____

Word Collectors:

5. Did you find the chapter's special word? Write it below:

_____

Now, collect three other words you learned from this chapter by writing them below!

6. _____ 7. _____ 8. _____

Narrate or write the meaning of the words you have found:

9. _____

_____

_____

10. _____

_____

_____

11. _____

_____

_____

MAP ADVENTURES

Name _____

America After WWI. Using a marker or crayon, color in the states where violence happened in the following list of places. Then add the numbers of the list to the appropriate states. See map on page 71 of the student book for answers.

1. Montgomery, Alabama
2. Bisbee, Arizona
3. El Dorado, Arkansas
4. Elaine, Arkansas
5. San Francisco, California
6. New London, Connecticut
7. Wilmington, Delaware
8. Lake City, Florida
9. Cadwell, Georgia
10. Dublin, Georgia
11. Hawkinsville, Georgia
12. Jenkins Co., Georgia
13. Macon, Georgia

14. Milan, Georgia
15. Warrenton, Georgia
16. Chicago, Illinois
17. Corbin, Kentucky
18. Bogalusa, Louisiana
19. Ellisville, Mississippi
20. Vicksburg, Mississippi
21. Omaha, Nebraska
22. Charleston, South Carolina
23. Knoxville, Tennessee
24. Longview, Texas
25. Norfolk, Virginia
26. Washington, D.C.

1. Using this image as a guide, write catalog text showing this new dress style with descriptions for someone looking to buy the latest fashions!

_____

_____

_____

_____

_____

2. Why was the Red Summer of 1919 such a violent one?

_____

_____

_____

3. What was it like for farmers once the war ended?

_____

_____

_____

4. What trial made the town of Dayton, TN famous?

_____

_____

_____

5. Why was the trial a turning point in history and for schools?

_____

_____

_____

MY TIMELINE!

Name _____

America After WWI. Pretend that you are Calvin Coolidge. You have just become president. What are some of the challenges facing the country in the 1920s? Write a letter to the American people explaining some of the issues the country is battling and what you think should be done about them.

_____

_____

_____

_____

_____

_____

_____

_____

_____

_____

_____

_____

_____

_____

_____

_____

_____

_____

_____

_____

_____

_____

_____

_____

My Timeline Manipulative. A timeline is a way to organize events of history in a logical, chronological way. If you would like to make this timeline element a part of a student's lesson, take some time to look over the important events of the current chapter. When creating their timeline, students can use sketches provided in the back of this Teacher Guide on pages 335–341. They may also choose to draw their own historical images or find them online. Use the timeline chart from the back and add information with each new lesson.

8 CRASH!

Materials needed for this chapter:

- ✔ Student Activity Pages
- ✔ Pencil/eraser
- ✔ Colored pencils or crayons
- ✔ Globe and/or atlas
- ✔ Optional: Books or websites about the stock market or its crashes

Oral Narration Questions and Answers

Q. Describe how the stock market and investing works.

A. Be sure the student can discuss the process, as well as the pros and cons of investments versus savings.

Q. Retell why the stock market crashed in 1929.

A. During the student's narration, make sure that the student doesn't simply focus on the impact of the crash, but on the events and actions that led to it as well.

Optional Digging Deeper

- ✔ This is a wonderful opportunity to start teaching fiscal responsibility. Does your student earn an allowance for doing chores? What happens to this money? Learn about the importance of saving as well as exploring the stock market.

Written Narration Idea for Older Students:

America is a place where people can live out their dreams — owning a business, inventing things, etc. Why is it important that you learn how to manage your money wisely? Were some of the decisions people made before the stock market crash wise? Why or why not?

_____

_____

_____

_____

_____

_____

_____

_____

SKETCHING

Name _____

Crash! Here is an example of a stock certificate for a new company you have created. Remember what things people were doing in the 1920s and base your business on this information. Fill in the blanks for company name, location of company, price for one share of stock, a set of letters that represents your company on the stock ticker, and your name as company president.

Company Name

Location of Company

Number of Shares

Price Per Share

Stock Ticker Name

Company President

1. What will you use the money for in your company from the sale of stock?

_____

_____

_____

2. What do you think will happen when the stock market crash happens and people start selling your stock for less than it is worth?

_____

_____

_____

3. What was the attraction of buying stocks during this period of history?

_____

_____

_____

Do the Math!

4. What was the average weekly salary for Americans before and after WWI?

_____

_____

_____

5. What conditions made it seem like buying stock was not risky?

_____

_____

_____

6. You have $200 saved and you want to buy stocks. You could buy 10 shares of Runaway Railroad stock worth $20 each. Or you could buy 100 shares if you take out a loan. How much would the bank have to loan you to buy that many shares of stock (minus what you already have)?

_____

_____

_____

MAP ADVENTURES

Name _____

Crash! There are many stock exchanges in America and around the world. Many have a regional focus. Based on their placement on this map, name the stock exchanges with each focus. (See map on pages 80–81 of the student book):

1. Agriculture:

_____

_____

2. Mining:

_____

_____

3. Local businesses:

_____

_____

A Big Crash!

4. It's Black Tuesday and your stock is worth much less than it was yesterday. Do you sell your stock at a loss or keep it and hope things gets better?

_____

_____

_____

5. How did Black Tuesday impact banks?

_____

_____

_____

6. What's the difference between a bull and bear market?

_____

_____

_____

Word Collectors:

7. This chapter's special word is_____.

List three other words you learned from this chapter.

8. _____ 9. _____ 10. _____

11. Can you explain their meaning?

_____

_____

_____

MY TIMELINE!

Crash! Pretend that you are at the New York Stock Exchange as the stock market crashes in 1929. You could be a stockbroker or a stock investor or a bystander. Describe in a diary entry what you witnessed.

_____

_____

_____

_____

_____

_____

_____

_____

_____

_____

_____

_____

_____

_____

_____

_____

_____

_____

_____

_____

_____

My Timeline Manipulative. A timeline is a way to organize events of history in a logical, chronological way. If you would like to make this timeline element a part of a student's lesson, take some time to look over the important events of the current chapter. When creating their timeline, students can use sketches provided in the back of this Teacher Guide on pages 335–341. They may also choose to draw their own historical images or find them online. Use the timeline chart from the back and add information with each new lesson.

9 THE GREAT DEPRESSION

Materials needed for this chapter:

✔ Student Activity Pages

✔ Pencil/eraser

✔ Colored pencils or crayons

✔ Globe and/or atlas

✔ Optional: Books or websites about the Great Depression, the CCC, or the Dust Bowl

Oral Narration Questions and Answers

Q. Tell what you learned about life during the Great Depression.

A. Allow your student to retell what he or she learned today. Encourage him or her to elaborate on the details of not just the country but of individuals as well.

Q. Talk about what you learned about the Dust Bowl.

A. Be sure the student understands and can discuss the cause of the tragedy and how people responded to it.

Optional Digging Deeper

✔ Look for local projects that have a connection to the CCC or other groups. Check your local historical society. It would be helpful for the comprehension of this chapter's concepts and issues to bring them down to your state. I recommend taking the time to do some research about what was happening in your state during this time period. Were there any special project sites there?

Written Narration Idea for Older Students:

Are there any CCC projects in your state? If so, what are they?

_____

_____

_____

_____

_____

_____

_____

_____

SKETCHING

Name _____

The Great Depression. Imagine that a CCC camp is being placed in your hometown. Here is what the plans for a CCC camp barrack looked like in Colorado. Can you recreate this plan for the new CCC camp?

Note: A datum line is a line that stands as a reference point.

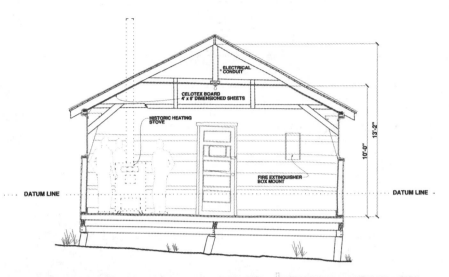

1. What was the economic situation in America during this time?

_____

_____

_____

2. What was a bank run?

_____

_____

_____

Copywork. America during the Great Depression was hurting. Many people were angry. Two presidents favored very different approaches to fixing it.

> **Economic depression cannot be cured by legislative action or executive pronouncement. Economic wounds must be healed by…the producers and consumers themselves.**
> **—Herbert Hoover**

_____

_____

_____

_____

> **Do something. If it works, do more of it. If it doesn't, do something else.**
> **—FDR**

_____

_____

_____

MAP ADVENTURES

Name _____

The Great Depression. This is a map of railroads in Texas in 1926. Look carefully at the map and remember this was the time before there were a lot of roads. If you had no money and were looking for work, the railroad offered an opportunity to move around the country — if you didn't get caught and thrown off the train.

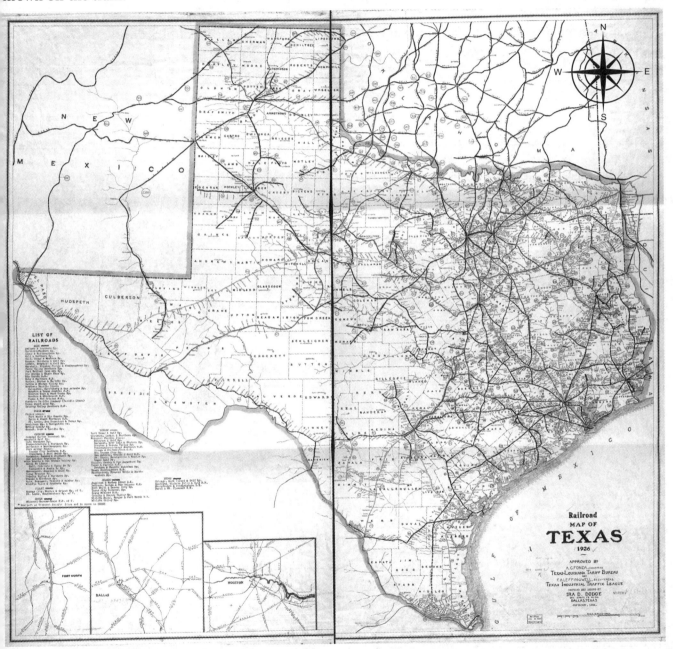

1. Which portion of the state had the most railroad connections — east or west? _____

2. Why was it important to choose a railroad with a lot of connection options?

_____

_____

_____

3. What was the nickname for many men and boys riding trains across the country during the Great Depression? Why were they on the trains?

_____

_____

_____

4. It was not an easy life for these men and boys. They had to live a rough and sometimes hungry life. Here one is preparing to make turtle soup. Imagine you are in a hobo camp and you are writing a short letter home about what this life is like.

_____

_____

_____

_____

_____

_____

Word Collectors:

5. Did you find the chapter's special word? Write it: _____

List three other words you learned from this chapter.

6. _____ 7. _____ 8. _____

Make sure you can explain the words to your teacher.

The Great Depression. Pretend that you are a reporter assigned to write about the Dust Bowl. You need to interview the Okies who are leaving for California. Write a newspaper article where you describe the conditions they were facing and their experiences once they reached California.

_____

_____

_____

_____

_____

_____

_____

_____

_____

_____

_____

_____

_____

_____

_____

_____

_____

_____

My Timeline Manipulative. A timeline is a way to organize events of history in a logical, chronological way. If you would like to make this timeline element a part of a student's lesson, take some time to look over the important events of the current chapter. When creating their timeline, students can use sketches provided in the back of this Teacher Guide on pages 335–341. They may also choose to draw their own historical images or find them online. Use the timeline chart from the back and add information with each new lesson.

10 THE WORLD AT WAR

Materials needed for this chapter:

- ✔ Student Activity Pages
- ✔ Pencil/eraser
- ✔ Colored pencils or crayons
- ✔ Globe and/or atlas
- ✔ Optional: Books or websites about Pearl Harbor

Oral Narration Questions and Answers

Q. Talk about what was happening in Europe.

A. Allow your student to retell what he or she learned today about the complex and volatile situation in Europe before American involvement with World War II, with some nations aggressively overtaking others.

Q. Retell what we have learned today about the Pearl Harbor attack.

A. Allow your student to tell you what stood out to him or her from the account of the attack. Be sure he or she can articulate why it was so traumatic for the American people and how the nation chose to respond.

Optional Digging Deeper

- ✔ You may want to encourage your student to research the attack on Pearl Harbor. There are many actual photographs taken during the attack. Please be aware that some of the photos show the casualties inflicted by the Japanese that day. The memorial for the attack located at the site of the *Arizona* is also interesting — there are many poignant news stories regarding it and World War II vets visiting it.

Written Narration Idea for Older Students:

America was reluctant to join the conflict of World War II. Why was this, and how did the attack at Pearl Harbor help unite the country in support of the war effort?

_____

_____

_____

_____

_____

_____

_____

_____

MAP ADVENTURES

Name _____

The World at War.

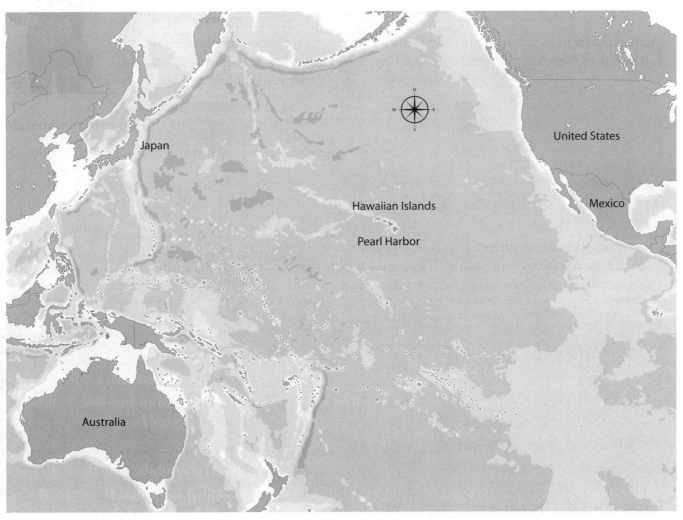

Japan

United States

Hawaiian Islands

Mexico

Pearl Harbor

Australia

1. Looking at the map above, why was the attack on Pearl Harbor both shocking and terrifying for Americans?

   _____

   _____

   _____

Between the Lines!

Read the following page, which includes President Roosevelt's address to Congress following the attack. Take a marker and find answers to the following questions:

2. Was Pearl Harbor the only site of the surprise attack by the Japanese? _____

3. Where else were attacks made?

_____

_____

_____

4. What actions had Japan taken to make America think that it wanted peace?

_____

_____

_____

5. Who declares war — the president or the Congress — in the United States?

_____

6. What was the date of the speech? _____

Copywork. Copy the following excerpts from this famous speech:

> **With confidence in our armed forces — with the unbounding determination**
> **of our people — we will gain the inevitable triumph — so help us God.**
> **—FDR**

_____

_____

_____

President Roosevelt's Joint Address to Congress
Leading to a Declaration of War Against Japan (1941)

Mr. Vice President, and Mr. Speaker, and Members of the Senate and House of Representatives:

Yesterday, December 7, 1941 — a date which will live in infamy — the United States of America was suddenly and deliberately attacked by naval and air forces of the Empire of Japan.

The United States was at peace with that Nation and, at the solicitation of Japan, was still in conversation with its Government and its Emperor looking toward the maintenance of peace in the Pacific. Indeed, one hour after Japanese air squadrons had commenced bombing in the American Island of Oahu, the Japanese Ambassador to the United States and his colleague delivered to our Secretary of State a formal reply to a recent American message. And while this reply stated that it seemed useless to continue the existing diplomatic negotiations, it contained no threat or hint of war or of armed attack.

It will be recorded that the distance of Hawaii from Japan makes it obvious that the attack was deliberately planned many days or even weeks ago. During the intervening time the Japanese Government has deliberately sought to deceive the United States by false statements and expressions of hope for continued peace.

The attack yesterday on the Hawaiian Islands has caused severe damage to American naval and military forces. I regret to tell you that very many American lives have been lost. In addition American ships have been reported torpedoed on the high seas between San Francisco and Honolulu.

Yesterday the Japanese Government also launched an attack against Malaya.

Last night Japanese forces attacked Hong Kong.

Last night Japanese forces attacked Guam.

Last night Japanese forces attacked the Philippine Islands.

Last night the Japanese attacked Wake Island. And this morning the Japanese attacked Midway Island.

Japan has, therefore, undertaken a surprise offensive extending throughout the Pacific area. The facts of yesterday and today speak for themselves. The people of the United States have already formed their opinions and well understand the implications to the very life and safety of our Nation.

As Commander in Chief of the Army and Navy I have directed that all measures be taken for our defense.

But always will our whole Nation remember the character of the onslaught against us.

No matter how long it may take us to overcome this premeditated invasion, the American people in their righteous might will win through to absolute victory. I believe that I interpret the will of the Congress and of the people when I assert that we will not only defend ourselves to the uttermost but will make it very certain that this form of treachery shall never again endanger us.

Hostilities exist. There is no blinking at the fact that our people, our territory, and our interests are in grave danger.

With confidence in our armed forces — with the unbounding determination of our people — we will gain the inevitable triumph — so help us God.

I ask that the Congress declare that since the unprovoked and dastardly attack by Japan on Sunday, December 7, 1941, a state of war has existed between the United States and the Japanese Empire.

Transcription courtesy of the Franklin D. Roosevelt Presidential Library and Museum; http://www. ourdocuments.gov/doc.php?doc=73&page=transcript; U.S. National Archives and Records Administration.

Sometimes we forget that people like our president have to work hard in times of trouble to say the right things. Here is a page from this famous speech with the editing marks included. The Library of Congress is just one source for important and interesting historical documents. The various presidential libraries and the national archives also have wonderful information. State and local archives can be fun to research as well!

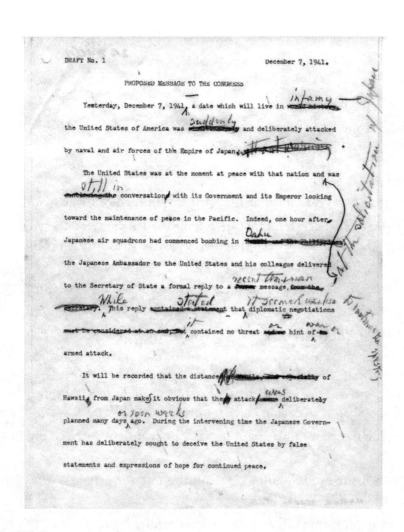

SKETCHING

Name _____

The World at War. You are on assignment as a news reporter to do a short article on the attack at Pearl Harbor. You will also need a sketch that goes with it — either of a map, image, or other related event (FDR's speech, declaration of war by Congress, the relocation of Japanese Americans, etc.) to go with your story. Write your story below and sketch your image in the box.

1. Why were Japanese Americans relocated to internment camps during World War II?

_____

_____

_____

_____

_____

_____

2. The internment camps may have been a reaction to the fear from the Pearl Harbor attack, but it was the wrong reaction (and a terrible one) for a nation built on the ideals of justice and freedom. Do you think the internment of Japanese Americans did anything to really help America win the war? Why or why not?

_____

_____

_____

Word Collectors:

3. Did you find the chapter's special word? Write it below:

_____

Now, collect three other words you learned from this chapter by writing them below!

4. _____ 5. _____ 6. _____

Make sure you can explain the words to your teacher.

MY TIMELINE!

Name _____

The World at War. Pretend that you are an American who has just learned about the Pearl Harbor attacks over the radio. Write a letter to a relative or friend describing what you know and what you are thinking and feeling.

_____

_____

_____

_____

_____

_____

_____

_____

_____

_____

_____

_____

_____

_____

_____

_____

_____

_____

_____

_____

My Timeline Manipulative. A timeline is a way to organize events of history in a logical, chronological way. If you would like to make this timeline element a part of a student's lesson, take some time to look over the important events of the current chapter. When creating their timeline, students can use sketches provided in the back of this Teacher Guide on pages 335–341. They may also choose to draw their own historical images or find them online. Use the timeline chart from the back and add information with each new lesson.

ARTIST STUDY

Name _____

Frank Lloyd Wright (Architect). The most famous American architect, Frank Lloyd Wright, was born in Wisconsin in 1867. By the 1880s, he was designing buildings, and he remained an active architect until his death in 1959.

(PD-US)

His career spanned seven decades, but he remains best known for his Prairie-style homes and his support for so-called organic architecture. One of the most important influences on Wright's style was his belief that American architecture should be uniquely American and not draw on European traditions. His Prairie homes were low and broad, an intentional design feature that drew inspiration from the landscape of the Great Plains. Other influences on his work included ancient Mayan architecture and Japanese art, which he collected.

The guiding force of his philosophy about organic architecture was that buildings should blend in with their environments and appear to be a natural part of them. He also preferred to use materials that were native to the area. Therefore, his homes built in the Midwestern prairies looked a lot different from his houses built in the Southwest deserts.

His most famous home design is Fallingwater, which is dramatically located over a waterfall. But he built many other well-known homes. Over 400 of his buildings are still standing across the United States and around the world.

Examples of Architecture by Frank Lloyd Wright

Nathan G. Moore House, Oak Park, IL, USA (J. Crocker)

Frederick C. Robie House (CC BY-SA 3.0)

More Examples of Architecture by Frank Lloyd Wright

Solomon R. Guggenheim Museum (Sailko, CC BY-SA 3.0)

Fallingwater (Sxenko, CC BY-SA 3.0)

Taliesin West, Scottsdale, Arizona (I, Gobeirne, CC BY-SA 3.0)

Choose one of the following activities to understand more about Frank Lloyd Wright's work.

1. You can either journal about or answer one or more of the following questions.

   ✔ Why do you think Wright thought it was so important for American architecture to be unique?

   ✔ Wright believed in the importance of organic architecture that blended in with the surroundings. Think about the landscapes where you live. What design elements would blend in and look natural?

2. Do an art assessment.

   ✔ What is the first thing you notice when you look at Wright's buildings?

   ✔ Which of these buildings is your favorite? Why?

   ✔ Why do you think he designed Fallingwater over a waterfall?

   ✔ What design elements do you see in common in his buildings? What design elements differ between them?

3. Try it!

   ✔ Use graph paper to draw your own building. Be sure to take some time to think of the landscape it will exist in. It can be like where you live or like somewhere you have never been before. You'll also need to keep in mind what the building will be used for — is it a home or an office building or a museum or something else? Once you have decided where it will be and what it will be, draw out each level and every room. Don't forget to sketch the outside, too!

11 AMERICA AT WAR, PART ONE

Materials needed for this chapter:

- ✔ Student Activity Pages
- ✔ Pencil/eraser
- ✔ Colored pencils or crayons
- ✔ Globe and/or atlas
- ✔ Optional: Books or websites about a soldier's life during World War II; depending on the location of their wartime service, there will be a wide range of experiences to explore.

Oral Narration Questions and Answers

Q. Talk about the strategies America used during World War II.

A. America wanted to win, but they needed a plan. Make sure the student can articulate which areas of the conflict were given first priority and what plans were made for future fighting in other regions of the conflict.

Q. Retell what you learned today about World War II.

A. Allow your student to tell you what stood out to him or her from the chapter. It really was a global conflict with areas both east and west of the United States as warzones.

Optional Digging Deeper

- ✔ Perhaps this would be a good time in your student's life to actually put his or her respect and honor into action. I highly recommend that you find an outlet of service for your student (and your whole family!) to do something nice in thanks for the people who have fought for our country.

Written Narration Idea for Older Students:

What made the war in the Pacific such a challenge for America?

_____

_____

_____

_____

_____

_____

_____

_____

SKETCHING

Name _____

America at War, Part One. Use this image to sketch your own image of this Japanese bomber.

1. Why did the U.S. choose to first focus on the war in Europe?

_____

_____

_____

The troops were headed to war and they needed tools that would help them win. Here at home people served in various jobs focused on civil defense. When unknown planes were sighted, charts like this one were used to determine what kind of plane it was — and then if it was a friend or foe.

Based on this chart, identify the following types of German war planes:

2. _____

3. _____

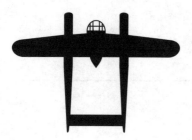

4. _____

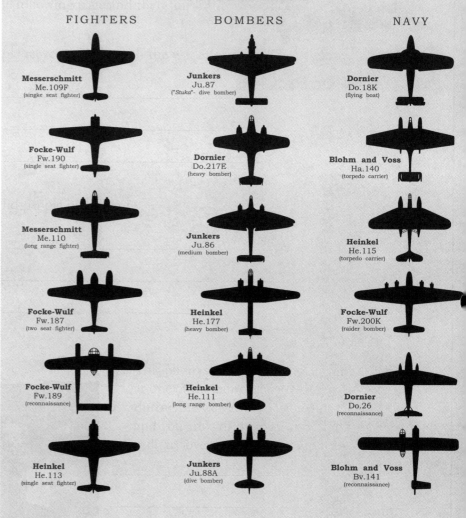

5. _____

MAP ADVENTURES

Name _____

America at War, Part One. Proposed map of U.S. bases taking into account the distance a long-range bomber of the time could fly to a target and return.

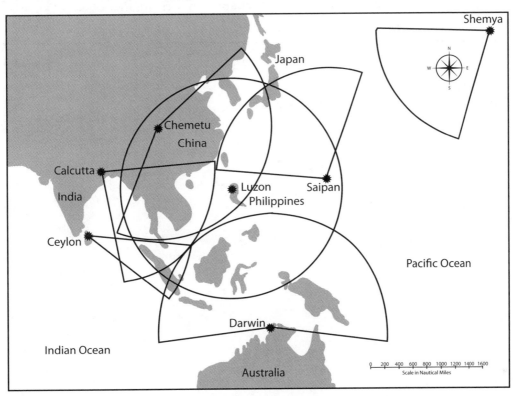

1. How does this map show the reasoning behind "island hopping" in the Pacific?

   _____

   _____

2. Who won in the Battle of the Coral Sea?

   _____

   _____

   _____

3. Why was the Battle of Midway such an important battle?

   _____

   _____

   _____

Word Collectors:

4. Have you found the chapter's special word? Write it below:

    _____

Now, collect three other words you learned from this chapter by writing them below!

5. _____   6. _____   7. _____

Use each word in a separate sentence for your teacher.

MY TIMELINE!

Name _____

America at War, Part One. Pretend that you are an American soldier or marine who is part of the island-hopping campaigns in the Pacific. What do you think about this strategy? Do you think this is a good way to end the war against Japan? Write a diary entry describing your thoughts on the subject.

_____
_____
_____
_____
_____
_____
_____
_____
_____
_____
_____
_____
_____
_____
_____
_____
_____
_____
_____

My Timeline Manipulative. A timeline is a way to organize events of history in a logical, chronological way. If you would like to make this timeline element a part of a student's lesson, take some time to look over the important events of the current chapter. When creating their timeline, students can use sketches provided in the back of this Teacher Guide on pages 335–341. They may also choose to draw their own historical images or find them online. Use the timeline chart from the back and add information with each new lesson.

12 AMERICA AT WAR, PART TWO

Dear Parent or Teacher,

At the end of this chapter, discuss with your student the importance of remembering and honoring the heroes of our country. Those who have given so much to ensure our freedom should be treated with the greatest respect and dignity.

Materials needed for this chapter:

- ✔ Student Activity Pages
- ✔ Pencil/eraser
- ✔ Colored pencils or crayons
- ✔ Globe and/or atlas
- ✔ Optional: There are a lot of ways to study more about World War II. You can focus either on different countries, different branches of the service, individual soldiers, civil defense, prisoner of war camps in America, partisans (people fighting against their own governments during the war), spies, technology, or heroes who sacrificed everything fighting for others.

Oral Narration Questions and Answers

Q. Talk about the battles you learned about today.

A. Allow your student to retell what he or she learned today. Ask about the battles America and its allies were winning and losing.

Q. Talk about how World War II ended.

A. World War II ended much differently than World War I did. Make sure the student can articulate what major events led to the end of conflict in both the Atlantic and Pacific war theaters.

Optional Digging Deeper

- ✔ Children are always affected by war, whether here in America or within the frontline battles of Asia and Europe. Discover how these conflicts affected children in different countries around the world. Or read stories or books about children who survived the Nazis, the atomic bombs, or those children who were part of the war effort here in America.

  Please be aware that any internet search or materials about Nazis, the Holocaust, or the use of atomic weapons could have very disturbing content for young children. It is important to prescreen any materials you are adding to make sure they are appropriate for the sensitivity and age of your student. There are age-appropriate sources available.

Written Narration Idea for Older Students:

Do you know a WWII veteran? If so, do you know any of his or her stories? Does anyone in your family know about his or her experiences?

_____

_____

_____

_____

_____

_____

_____

_____

SKETCHING

Name _____

America at War, Part Two. This is an example of some of the meals that American soldiers had to eat when they were given rations. The packaging is very plain.

Pretend that you work in a company that provides chocolate bars to the military. Can you design a wrapper for the chocolate that is a little more fun and creative? Remember, it's important to let the soldiers know the following info on the wrapper:

- ✔ What it is
- ✔ How much there is
- ✔ And some encouraging words!

1. Imagine you are in America and you get a letter from a family member serving in Europe during the war. He is describing a meal just like the one pictured on the previous page. Answer his letter, describing what you are having for dinner.

_____

_____

_____

_____

2. By the time the war in Europe ended, the astonishing extent of the horrors perpetrated by German Nazis was revealed. Who were among their victims?

_____

_____

_____

3. After years of fighting, what was the situation in many parts of Europe for civilians?

_____

_____

_____

4. Why did America choose not to invade Japan after all the "island hopping" to get there?

_____

_____

_____

_____

Copywork. Copy the following quote from General George Patton:

Courage is fear holding on a minute longer.

_____

_____

MAP ADVENTURES

Name _____

America at War, Part Two. If you want to see this map in color, look on page 121 in your student book. This shows what a challenge it was for America in trying to attack Japan.

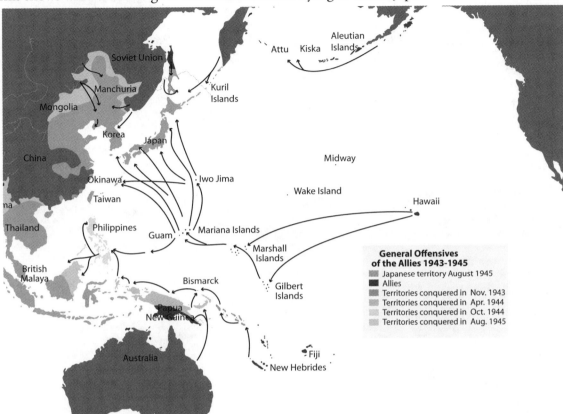

On this copy of the map, use a colored marker to:

1. Circle the islands of Kiska and Attu.

2. Draw a square around Midway and Wake Islands.

3. Draw a triangle around the Philippines.

Answer the following questions:

1. Which is closer to Japan, Midway or Guam? _____

2. Which is closer to Australia, the Philippines or New Hebrides? _____

3. Attu and Kiska are part of what island group, Gilbert or Aleutian? _____

4. Which is closer to the mainland of China, Iwo Jima or Okinawa? _____

5. List the names of the allied countries on the map as of 1945:

    a. _____   b. _____

    c. _____   d. _____

    e. _____   f. _____

Word Collectors:

6. Did you find the chapter's special word? Write it below:

_____

Now, collect three other words you learned from this chapter by writing them below!

7. _____   8. _____   9. _____

Narrate the meaning of the words you have found.

MY TIMELINE!

America at War, Part Two. The Allied invasion of Normandy on D-Day is one of the most famous battles in history, but one aspect of it that a lot of people don't know about is the Ghost Army. This army was important to the success of the Allied plan, but the Ghost Army was not an army at all! It was created to distract the Germans and mislead them about where the invasion would be. Even after D-Day, the Ghost Army was sent in to continue confusing the Germans. The Ghost Army had inflatable tanks, rubber planes, fake secret codes, and even actors who pretended to be soldiers and famous generals.

Pretend that you are a member of the Ghost Army. What is your job? How did it help the war effort? Right now, your work is top secret and cannot be revealed, so write an account of your experiences that will be published after the war is over!

_____

_____

_____

_____

_____

_____

_____

_____

_____

_____

_____

_____

_____

_____

_____

_____

_____

_____

_____

_____

My Timeline Manipulative. A timeline is a way to organize events of history in a logical, chronological way. If you would like to make this timeline element a part of a student's lesson, take some time to look over the important events of the current chapter. When creating their timeline, students can use sketches provided in the back of this Teacher Guide on pages 335–341. They may also choose to draw their own historical images or find them online. Use the timeline chart from the back and add information with each new lesson.

13 LIFE ON THE HOMEFRONT

Dear Parent or Teacher,

One thing to remember to remind your students about the homefront during WWII is that historians tend to focus on what was different from years past. That is why the student book focuses on women who worked in factories and joined the military during the war. This was different from past wars.

Nevertheless, the majority of American women were still homemakers and stay-at-home mothers during WWII. Of the approximately 30,000,000 women who met the age requirements for joining the service, less than 2% did. The rates of female workers did increase significantly. In 1939, approximately 25% of adult American women worked outside the home. Within 5 years, that percentage had increased by about 12%. But that meant that nearly ⅔ of women still did not work outside the home, and that was even more true of mothers of small children. Only about 10% of them worked outside the home during the war years, not much more than in years past.

These women who stayed home contributed substantially to the war effort through growing victory gardens, volunteering in their communities, and providing stable home environments for their families during a difficult time.

Materials needed for this chapter:

✔ Student Activity Pages

✔ Pencil/eraser

✔ Colored pencils or crayons; glue/tape

✔ Globe and/or atlas

✔ Optional: Books or websites about the American homefront during WWII

Oral Narration Questions and Answers

Q. Tell what you learned about the homefront.

A. Be sure the student can give some details about how the war impacted both people and the economy during the war years. See if he or she can also share about the experience of women and African Americans.

Q. Talk about what you learned today about the homefront.

A. Allow your student to retell what he or she learned today. Encourage him or her to elaborate on the details of what Americans were doing at that time for the war effort, including that of Japanese Americans.

Optional Digging Deeper

✔ What role did children have during WWII? In what ways were they depended upon to help? What is a victory garden? Help your student find the answers to these questions. Learn about the way the country pulled together to conserve and recycle our resources during the war.

Written Narration Idea for Older Students:

1. Women worked in factories and helped keep our country running during WWII. Women had similar experiences in World War I. How were the experiences for women different in WWII than WWI?

_____

_____

_____

_____

_____

_____

_____

_____

_____

Word Collectors:

2. Did you find the chapter's special word? Write it below:

    _____

Now, collect three other words you learned from this chapter by writing them below!

3. _____   4. _____   5. _____

Narrate the meaning of the words you have found.

SKETCHING

Name _____

Life on the Homefront. Here is an example of a poster encouraging people to plant victory gardens on the homefront during WWII. Children were often responsible for planting and helping to maintain the gardens. This provided extra food here at home while supplies were being sent overseas for American military personnel.

It's time your neighborhood started planting some victory gardens. Create a poster encouraging others to make one. Be sure to make it bright and colorful. And remind them how important it is for the war effort!

1. How many fighting men did the draft bring in for the war effort?

_____

_____

_____

2. What were the factories of America producing at this time?

_____

_____

_____

3. Who were the workers in American factories with many men serving overseas?

_____

_____

_____

4. What was it like to serve in the war as an African American during this time?

_____

_____

_____

_____

_____

MAP ADVENTURES

Name _____

Life on the Homefront. Soldiers of the soil, it's time to dig! In the square below, design your own victory garden. Follow the following suggestions if you like!

Three rows of corn	Two rows of onions	Half a row of peppers
Three rows of green beans	Two rows of beets	Half a row of radishes
Three rows of potatoes	One row of peas	Half a row of spinach
Two rows of carrots	One row of squash	Half a row of cabbage

Be sure to label your rows!

1. What was rationing? What items were rationed during the war?

_____

_____

_____

Do the rations book project on the following page and then finish this worksheet.

2. What kinds of things did people recycle to help with the war effort?

_____

_____

_____

3. What were war bonds? Why did people buy them?

_____

_____

_____

4. This photo shows children planting a victory garden at one of the camps Japanese Americans were sent to during the war. Imagine you are a child at the camp and you are writing to your brother serving in the U.S. military overseas. Tell him about your victory garden.

_____

_____

_____

_____

_____

_____

_____

_____

Do Your Rations Book!

Cut out the following stamps and fill out your ration book on the back of this page. You need the following — and it tells how many stamps it will take for each:

- ✔ 1 pair of shoes – one aircraft carrier stamp
- ✔ 1 pound of sugar – four tank stamps
- ✔ 10 pounds of flour – five artillery stamps
- ✔ 5 gallons of gasoline – three fighter plane stamps

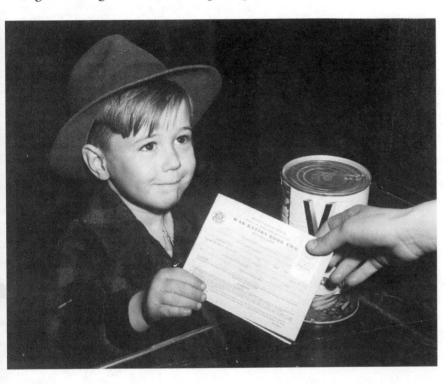

An eager school boy gets his first experience in using a War Ration Book. Photo by the United States Department of the Treasury.

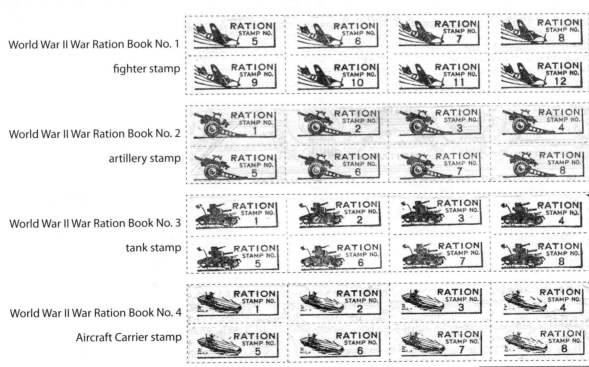

World War II War Ration Book No. 1

fighter stamp

World War II War Ration Book No. 2

artillery stamp

World War II War Ration Book No. 3

tank stamp

World War II War Ration Book No. 4

Aircraft Carrier stamp

My Ration Book

5 gallons of gasoline				
Three fighter plane stamps				

10 pounds of flour				
Five artillery stamps				

1 pound of sugar				
Four tank stamps				

1 pair of shoes				
One aircraft carrier stamp				

MY TIMELINE!

Name _____

Life on the Homefront. Pretend that you are one of the Japanese Americans living in an internment camp during World War II. What is it like to live in the internment camp? What do you think about the internment policy? Write a letter to a relative or friend outside the camp explaining your thoughts and feelings.

_____

_____

_____

_____

_____

_____

_____

_____

_____

_____

_____

My Timeline Manipulative. A timeline is a way to organize events of history in a logical, chronological way. If you would like to make this timeline element a part of a student's lesson, take some time to look over the important events of the current chapter. When creating their timeline, students can use sketches provided in the back of this Teacher Guide on pages 335–341. They may also choose to draw their own historical images or find them online. Use the timeline chart from the back and add information with each new lesson.

14 THE COLD WAR

Materials needed for this chapter:

- ✔ Student Activity Pages
- ✔ Pencil/eraser
- ✔ Glue/tape
- ✔ Scissors
- ✔ Colored pencils or crayons
- ✔ Globe and/or atlas
- ✔ Optional: Books or websites about the Cold War. The atomic bomb or atomic energy would be additional topics, but they are only appropriate for older, mature students!

Oral Narration Questions and Answers

Q. Talk about how America helped countries rebuild after the war.

A. Make sure the student can talk about the conditions in the countries where battles had been fought and lost. Encourage additional details if he or she has not mentioned the Marshall Plan or the roots of conflict with the Soviet Union.

Q. Tell what you learned about the Korean War.

A. See what details your student shares with you about the conflict. Make sure he or she understands how it fits within the concept of the Cold War.

Optional Digging Deeper

- ✔ Research how, when, and why the United Nations was formed.

Written Narration Idea for Older Students:

What was the Cold War, and what countries did it involve?

_____

_____

_____

_____

_____

_____

_____

_____

SKETCHING

Name _____

The Cold War. This label went on all aid packages that were sent out as part of the Marshall Plan. Recreate this label on the top box.

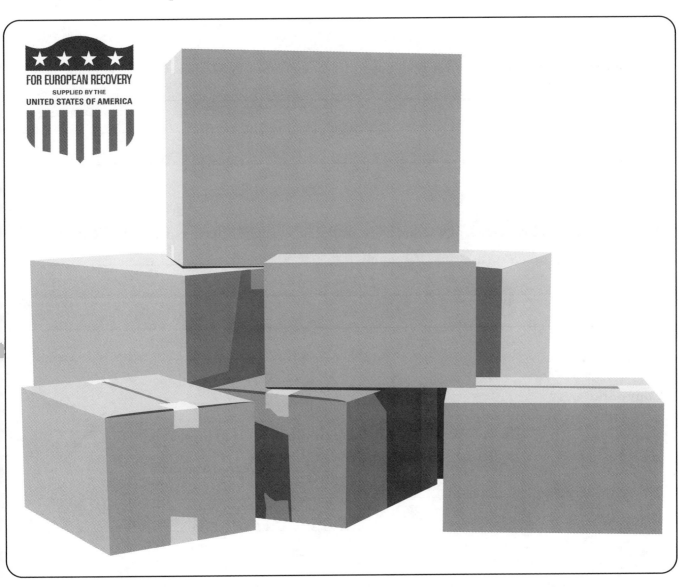

1. Just after World War II ended, what were American troops doing in Germany and Japan?

_____

_____

_____

2. Describe the Marshall Plan.

_____

_____

_____

3. Tell why so many Americans distrusted the Soviet Union even though they were allies during the war.

_____

_____

_____

4. Share why people being sick of war and a fear of atomic weapons helped to define the Cold War.

_____

_____

_____

Copywork:

The only way human beings can win a war is to prevent it.

—George Marshall

_____

_____

Don't fight the problem, decide it.

—George Marshall

_____

_____

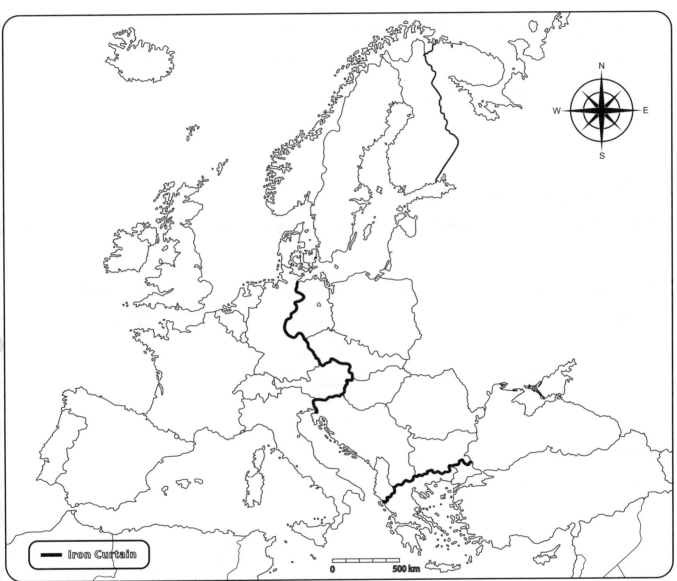

MAP ADVENTURES

Name _____

The Cold War. Color in red the areas that were part of the Soviet Union. (See map on page 140 of student book.)

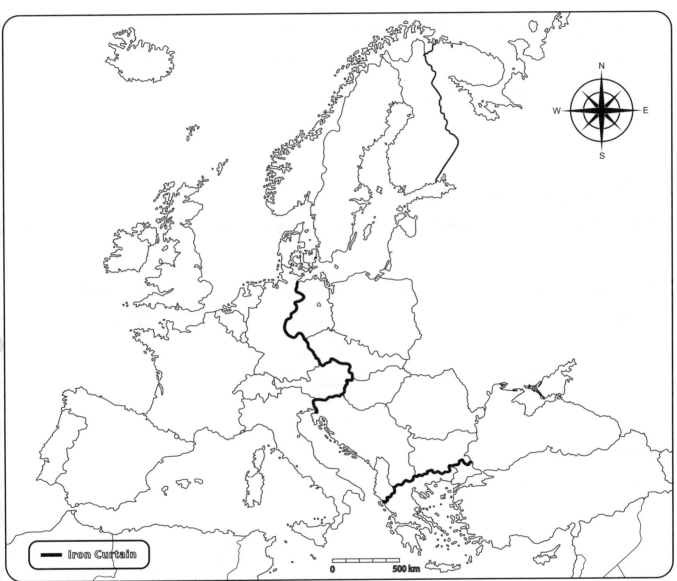

— **Iron Curtain**

0   500 km

1. Russia was trying to spread communism around the world. What actions did America take to prevent that?

_____

_____

_____

2. Tell what President Eisenhower's strategy was for Korea.

_____

_____

_____

_____

_____

_____

3. Why was the Berlin Airlift needed?

_____

_____

_____

_____

_____

_____

Word Collectors:

4. Did you find the chapter's special word? Write it below:

_____

Now, collect three other words you learned from this chapter by writing them below!

5. _____   6. _____   7. _____

Make sure you can explain the words to your teacher.

The Cold War. Pretend that you are living in 1950 when the United States enters the Korean War. What are your thoughts and feelings about this war? Do you agree with the decision to intervene? Why or why not? Write a letter to your local newspaper explaining your thoughts on the subject.

_____

_____

_____

_____

_____

_____

_____

_____

_____

_____

_____

_____

_____

_____

_____

_____

_____

_____

_____

_____

_____

_____

_____

My Timeline Manipulative. A timeline is a way to organize events of history in a logical, chronological way. If you would like to make this timeline element a part of a student's lesson, take some time to look over the important events of the current chapter. When creating their timeline, students can use sketches provided in the back of this Teacher Guide on pages 335–341. They may also choose to draw their own historical images or find them online. Use the timeline chart from the back and add information with each new lesson.

15 THE GOLDEN AGE OF AMERICA

Materials needed for this chapter:

✔ Student Activity Pages

✔ Pencil/eraser

✔ Colored pencils or crayons

✔ Globe and/or atlas

✔ Optional: Books or websites showing pictures of the beautiful cars of the 1950s and the historic Route 66. (There are more optional resource suggestions in the Digging Deeper section at the bottom of this page.)

Oral Narration Questions and Answers

Q. Discuss what you read about life in the 1950s.

A. Allow your student to narrate freely his or her favorite part of what he or she learned in this chapter. Discuss with your student several possibilities of enrichment opportunities, such as watching a movie made during this time period or listening to music.

Q. Talk about the challenges facing America in the 1950s.

A. American history is not a perfect one, but there are many opportunities to show that America changes for the better when needed. Take the time to discuss the concept of segregation mentioned in this section of the chapter and how it no longer exists today.

Optional Digging Deeper

✔ This time period has many fun aspects! There are many family friendly movies that were filmed during this time, and the music reflected the general atmosphere of the country — carefree and ready to move forward. Your student may enjoy watching one of the song-and-dance type movies made during this era. My family has enjoyed *Singing in the Rain, Anchors Away*, and *White Christmas*. Talk to your children early on in the week, and make plans for a family movie night or some other type of activity to bring this decade to life!

Written Narration Idea for Older Students:

How did life change in the 1950s?

_____

_____

_____

_____

_____

_____

_____

_____

MAP ADVENTURES

Name _____

The Golden Age of America. You lost your map on your cross-country trip — but don't worry, here is one you can complete! Take a colored marker and re-draw the Route 66 highway on it. See pages 150–151 in the student book.

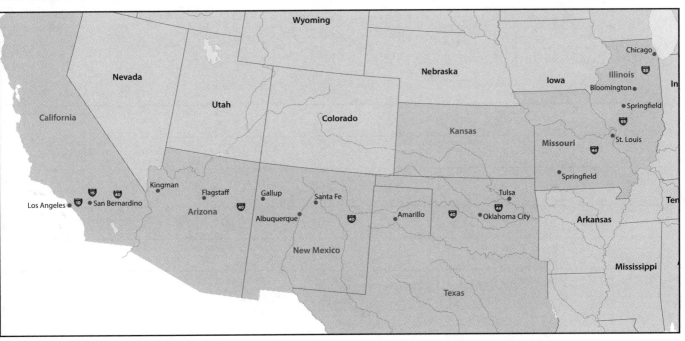

1. How did the popularity of cars help influence the culture of this decade?

_____

_____

_____

2. Describe what television was like in the 1950s — the shows, the actors, etc.

_____

_____

_____

_____

_____

_____

3. Can you name some of the popular movies of the time?

_____

_____

_____

4. Give details about the fashion of the 1950s.

_____

_____

_____

_____

_____

_____

Copywork:

Charlton Heston was a well-known actor in the 20th century. Here is what he had to say about his work as an actor:

> **I've played three presidents, three saints and two geniuses**
> **— and that's probably enough for any man.**
> **—Charlton Heston**

_____

_____

_____

SKETCHING

Name _____

The Golden Age of America. There is money to be made if you have a business along Route 66! You could own a hotel, a gas station, an Old West town, or other attraction. But you need a sign on the highway with the name of your business. Here is an outline for you to draw in to make your sign and also fill in your details:

1. The 1950s were not just about fun. There were many who lived in fear during the decade. Why?

_____

_____

_____

2. What was the Red Scare?

_____

_____

_____

3. Who was Senator Joe McCarthy?

_____

_____

_____

4. How was segregation implemented into American culture at this time in history?

_____

_____

_____

Word Collectors:

5. Have you found the chapter's special word? Write it below:

_____

Now, collect three other words you learned from this chapter by writing them below!

6. _____   7. _____   8. _____

Use each word in a separate sentence for your teacher.

9. **Prepping!** Fallout shelters stocked with food and other supplies were popular in the 1950s. Today, many people also prepare, or prep, for a disaster. Do you and your family have supplies of food, batteries, and water in case of a natural disaster or other emergency? What would you need?

_____

_____

_____

MY TIMELINE!

Name _____

The Golden Age of America. Pretend that you are a reporter driving along Route 66 in the 1950s. You are documenting your trip for your readers. What cities and locations do you want to make sure your readers know about? What stories do you have to tell from your trip? Write a newspaper article that covers your experiences.

_____

_____

_____

_____

_____

_____

_____

_____

_____

_____

_____

_____

_____

_____

_____

_____

_____

_____

_____

_____

_____

_____

My Timeline Manipulative. A timeline is a way to organize events of history in a logical, chronological way. If you would like to make this timeline element a part of a student's lesson, take some time to look over the important events of the current chapter. When creating their timeline, students can use sketches provided in the back of this Teacher Guide on pages 335–341. They may also choose to draw their own historical images or find them online. Use the timeline chart from the back and add information with each new lesson.

ARTIST STUDY

Name _____

Helen Frankenthaler (Abstract Expressionist). One of the most famous art movements to emerge in the 20th century was abstract expressionism. This style of art was developed in America, specifically in New York City, after World War II. These works were abstract in that they didn't usually depict a recognizable scene or person or thing. This was the first major school of painting developed in the United States, and it helped New York City become a leading center for art. Before, Europe — and especially Paris — had been perceived as the center of art.

One of the leading abstract expressionists was Helen Frankenthaler. Born in the 1920s in New York City to a wealthy Jewish family, Frankenthaler started her career in the 1950s. By this time, abstract expressionism was already a well-known school of painting. Like many abstract expressionists, she liked working on large areas of canvas, even covering the entire floor of a room with canvas.

She, however, also experimented with new techniques. She developed one called "soak-stain," in which she poured thinned paint onto a canvas and let it soak in. Though Frankenthaler's paintings were abstract, she drew a lot of inspiration from landscapes.

Frankenthaler also was particularly interested in the use of color and helped develop a unique offshoot from abstract expressionism called Color Field painting. This type of painting placed less emphasis on the brush movements many abstract expressionists used and instead focused on large, solid areas of color. Color field paintings were flat, meaning that the artists didn't want them to look 3-D.

Frankenthaler also developed an interest in printmaking and applied some of her painting techniques, including "soak-stain," to that field of art. She passed away in 2011.

Examples of Paintings by Helen Frankenthaler

50 Works on Paper (CC BY-SA 2.0)

50 Works on Paper (CC BY-SA 2.0)

Jacob's Ladder (CC BY 2.0)

Choose one of the following activities to understand more about Helen Frankenthaler's work.

1. You can either journal about or answer one or more of the following questions.
    - ✔ Why do you think abstract expressionism was so popular after World War II?
    - ✔ Why was it significant that the United States became a center for art in the 1900s?
    - ✔ Why do you think Color Field painters were so interested in making their paintings look flat?
    - ✔ Do you like abstract art? Why or why not?

2. Do an art assessment.
    - ✔ What is the first thing you notice when you look at Frankenthaler's paintings?
    - ✔ Which of these paintings is your favorite? Why?
    - ✔ What do you notice about the lines she uses in her art?
    - ✔ Can you detect her use of "soak-stain"? How so?

3. Try it!
    - ✔ With your parents' permission, try your own hand at abstract expressionism and soak-stain painting.
    - ✔ Gather plastic garbage bags, white paper, several colors of tempera paint, measuring spoons (tablespoons), small containers, and paintbrushes or sponges. You'll also need access to water.
    - ✔ Put down garbage bags to protect the workspace. Then select 3 different paint colors and measure 1 tablespoon each of water and tempera paint into 3 different containers.
    - ✔ Hold the paper underneath running water to evenly coat one side and then shake off the excess and press the paper flat onto the garbage bags.
    - ✔ Pour and drip the paint from the containers onto the paper. The colors will start to soak and stain the paper.
    - ✔ You can leave the painting as is, but you can also use paintbrushes or sponges, as Frankenthaler did, to move the paint around.

(Activity adapted from https://www.education.com/activity/article/poured-paint/)

16 TUMULTUOUS TIMES

Materials needed for this chapter:

✔ Student Activity Pages

✔ Pencil/eraser

✔ Colored pencils or crayons

✔ Globe and/or atlas

✔ Optional: Books or websites about segregation in the United States during the 1960s. I highly recommend the books *Little Rock Girl 1957* by Shelley Tougas and *The Story of Ruby Bridges* by Robert Coles.

Oral Narration Questions and Answers

Q. Retell and discuss what we have read so far.

A. Take the time to locate the places involved in the Cuban Missile Crisis. This was a scary time in our country's history! Take the time to discuss it with your student, finding the locations on a world map.

Q. Tell what you learned today about the Vietnam War.

A. Again, allow your student to tell what stood out to him or her from today's reading. Discuss any details you feel are important for your student to understand and remember.

Optional Digging Deeper

✔ If your student has not learned about the Cuban Missile Crisis, this would be great time to spend a little time researching and discussing it.

Written Narration Idea for Older Students:

1. Describe what the Peace Corps does and why President Kennedy created the organization. If you joined the Peace Corps, what country would you want to go to and what job would you want to try?

_____

_____

_____

_____

_____

_____

_____

_____

_____

Word Collectors:

2. Have you found the chapter's special word? Write it below:

_____

Now, collect three other words you learned from this chapter by writing them below!

3. _____   4. _____   5. _____

Use each word in a separate sentence for your teacher.

MAP ADVENTURES

Name _____

Tumultuous Times. These dashed lines show how far the different kinds of missiles from Cuba could reach targets in the United States. On the map draw a small house where you live. Then draw stars on your state capitol and on Washington D.C. Would you have been affected by the crisis? Would any of your family?

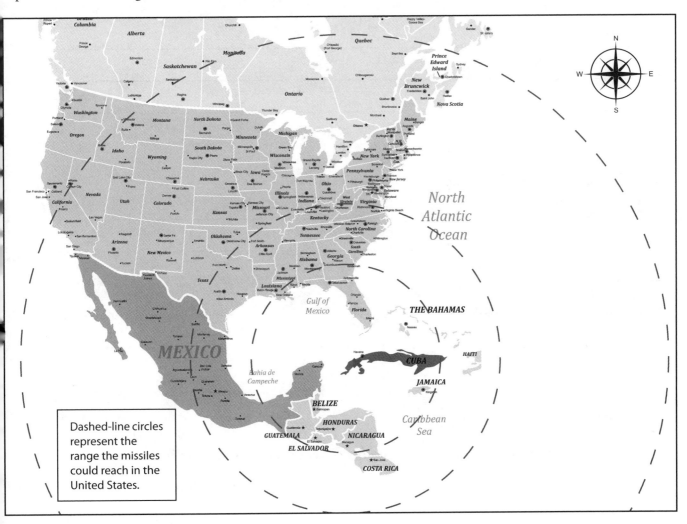

Dashed-line circles represent the range the missiles could reach in the United States.

Calculate it!

1. Take a ruler and consider every inch as 200 miles. How many inches is it from Cuba to your house?

_____

2. How many miles is this?

_____

3. What was the Cuban Missile Crisis?

_____

_____

_____

_____

_____

4. Why were the 1960s such a tumultuous time in America?

_____

_____

_____

_____

Copywork:

> **Ask not what your country can do for you; ask what you can do for your country.**
>
> **—President Kennedy**

_____

_____

_____

SKETCHING

Name _____

Tumultuous Times. President Kennedy had many dreams for making America even better, but he didn't have the chance to do them. Stamps are often issued in honor of historical people and events. Can you draw an image of President Kennedy for a commemorative stamp?

Angela's JFK   **My JFK**

1. What is communism?

_____

_____

_____

_____

2. Why did America become involved in the conflict in Vietnam?

_____

_____

_____

3. These are the kinds of helicopters that took American troops to locations in Vietnam. Can you imagine riding in one? What do you think it would have been like?

_____

_____

_____

4. What does it mean to be a good steward of what God has given us?

_____

_____

_____

Tumultuous Times. Pretend that you are living in 1962 and have just heard the announcement about the Supreme Court outlawing prayer in public school. Write a letter to the Supreme Court where you address your concerns with this decision.

_____

_____

_____

_____

_____

_____

_____

_____

_____

_____

_____

_____

_____

_____

_____

_____

_____

_____

_____

My Timeline Manipulative. A timeline is a way to organize events of history in a logical, chronological way. If you would like to make this timeline element a part of a student's lesson, take some time to look over the important events of the current chapter. When creating their timeline, students can use sketches provided in the back of this Teacher Guide on pages 335–341. They may also choose to draw their own historical images or find them online. Use the timeline chart from the back and add information with each new lesson.

17 CHANGING TIMES

Dear Parent or Teacher,

There are many controversial events and cultural fads during the 1970s. For example, the peace symbol is considered to be an iconic one of the decade and remains popular today. However, many people associate the symbol with the occult or with Nero's Cross (or Broken Cross) related to the suppression of Christianity during the Roman Empire. Much like the history of words, it is an example of how symbols can change over time. Originally it was a symbol for nuclear disarmament, then a counter-culture symbol of the '60s and '70s, an occult symbol, a peace symbol, or merely a decorative design. Because of the controversial nature of the symbol, we have limited its use in the student text to one small image — choosing not to highlight or connect it with activities or special features in this course. How much you choose to utilize the symbol in additional discussions — if any — either related to this decade or changing over time has been left to your discretion.

Materials needed for this chapter:

- ✔ Student Activity Pages
- ✔ Pencil/eraser
- ✔ Colored pencils or crayons
- ✔ Globe and/or atlas
- ✔ Optional: Books or websites about the space race. For older students, there are a number of good documentaries with actual footage of the people behind the scenes. Our family has enjoyed *Rocket Men*.

Oral Narration Questions and Answers

Q. Talk about some of the changes that happened in the 1960s.

A. Allow your student to retell what he or she learned today. See if he or she can give examples of the successes and challenges America faced.

Q. Tell what you learned today about the anti-war protests.

A. Take time to discuss the points your student makes to you about this. Protests can help highlight problems, but they need to be done the right way.

Optional Digging Deeper

- ✔ There are some wonderful, original video clips of the first man to walk on the moon. You may enjoy researching possible video clips for your student to view on YouTube™.

Written Narration Idea for Older Students:

What were some of the inventions and discoveries of the 1960s?

_____

_____

_____

_____

_____

_____

_____

_____

SKETCHING

Name _____

Changing Times. You just got a new job at a fashion magazine! It's time to talk about the fashion and protests of the 1960s in this new magazine. Create your magazine cover with the Top 5 stories of interest you have from reading this chapter. The names of the articles will be included on the cover along with a sketch you complete from this photo!

June 1968

ME! MAGAZINE

Draw this or similar image here ←

Put 5 article titles here ←

Word Collectors:

1. Did you find the chapter's special word? Write it below:

   _____

Now, collect three other words you learned from this chapter by writing them below!

2. _____ 3. _____ 4. _____

Narrate or write the meaning of the words you have found:

5. _____

   _____

6. _____

   _____

7. _____

   _____

8. How were fashions of the 1960s different from those of the 1950s?

   _____

   _____

   _____

MAP ADVENTURES

Name _____

Changing Times. Welcome to our Moon Mission! Use the space below to draw a map of your landing site on the moon. Enjoy your adventure!

1. What kinds of progress were happening in this decade?

_____

_____

_____

2. How were things different in America than in the past when it came to the draft for the Vietnam War?

_____

_____

_____

3. What Supreme Court decisions were made that represented a moral change for this time?

_____

_____

_____

Man on the Moon!

4. Imagine watching the news and realizing a man had walked on the moon. What would you have written for a news report on the event?

_____

_____

_____

_____

_____

_____

_____

MY TIMELINE!

Name _____

Changing Times. Pretend that it is 1969, and you have just watched Neil Armstrong walk on the moon. Write a letter to him telling him what it was like to watch him and what you were thinking and feeling. Be sure to ask him any questions you have about the moon!

_____

_____

_____

_____

_____

_____

_____

_____

_____

_____

_____

_____

_____

_____

_____

_____

_____

_____

_____

_____

My Timeline Manipulative. A timeline is a way to organize events of history in a logical, chronological way. If you would like to make this timeline element a part of a student's lesson, take some time to look over the important events of the current chapter. When creating their timeline, students can use sketches provided in the back of this Teacher Guide on pages 335–341. They may also choose to draw their own historical images or find them online. Use the timeline chart from the back and add information with each new lesson.

18 THE CIVIL RIGHTS MOVEMENT

Materials needed for this chapter:

✔ Student Activity Pages

✔ Pencil/eraser

✔ Colored pencils or crayons

✔ Globe and/or atlas

✔ Optional: Books or websites about Rosa Parks and Dr. Martin Luther King Jr. For upper elementary/
junior high students, I recommend *Rosa Parks: My Story* by Rosa Parks. For all students, the book
Martin's Big Words: The Life of Dr. Martin Luther King, Jr. by Doreen Rappaport.

Oral Narration Questions and Answers

Q. Discuss what happened during the Montgomery Bus Boycott.

A. Allow your student to share what caught his or her attention from the reading. Make sure he or she
has an understanding of why the boycott happened and how it only takes one person to make a big
difference in America.

Q. Tell what you learned about the Civil Rights Movement today.

A. Segregation is a difficult topic to teach and learn about. Discuss with your student the privileges he or
she enjoys that were not enjoyed by African American children during this time of our history.

Optional Digging Deeper

✔ You may want your older student to research a little more. You may want to assign a deeper reading
and writing assignment on a chosen Civil Rights Movement hero.

Written Narration Idea for Older Students:

Would you have had enough courage to do what Rosa Parks did? Why or why not?

_____

_____

_____

_____

_____

_____

_____

_____

_____

SKETCHING

Name _____

The Civil Rights Movement. Use crayons to color this map to match the one in your student book on pages 180–181. Now label the state where you live. What segregation laws existed in your state back then?

1. Tell what happened when African American students began attending schools that had been used only for white students.

   _____

   _____

   _____

2. What did Rosa Parks do that prompted the bus boycott?

   _____

   _____

3. Who was Dr. Martin Luther King Jr.?

_____

_____

_____

4. Why were there riots by African Americans at this time?

_____

_____

_____

Word Collectors:

5. Find the chapter's special word. Write it below:

_____

Now, collect three other words you learned from this chapter by writing them below!

6. _____   7. _____   8. _____

Be sure to explain the meaning of each word to your teacher.

MAP ADVENTURES

Name _____

The Civil Rights Movement. In America, the Declaration of Independence makes clear that every person is considered equal with important rights given to us by God — though at times in American history, this has not been the case in the lives of African Americans, Japanese Americans, or Native Americans by how they were treated or because of laws and policies made to restrict their freedom. What does the word "equality" mean to you? Can you draw a poster showing that in America we are all equal under the laws of the nation?

1. What were "Jim Crow" laws?

_____

_____

_____

2. How did Malcolm X and Dr. King differ on their approach to ending segregation and obtaining equal rights?

_____

_____

_____

_____

3. What issue did Freedom Summer focus on?

_____

_____

_____

_____

4. In Genesis, we read that God created Adam and Eve — one race, the human race. They are the first parents on earth and everyone today is one of their descendants. How can understanding this help us overcome racism?

_____

_____

_____

_____

_____

_____

MY TIMELINE! Name _____

The Civil Rights Movement. Pretend that you are a participant in the Montgomery bus boycott. Write a letter to a relative or friend explaining why the boycott is taking place, what you hope to achieve, and why it is important.

_____

_____

_____

_____

_____

_____

_____

_____

_____

_____

_____

_____

_____

_____

_____

_____

_____

_____

_____

_____

_____

_____

My Timeline Manipulative. A timeline is a way to organize events of history in a logical, chronological way. If you would like to make this timeline element a part of a student's lesson, take some time to look over the important events of the current chapter. When creating their timeline, students can use sketches provided in the back of this Teacher Guide on pages 335–341. They may also choose to draw their own historical images or find them online. Use the timeline chart from the back and add information with each new lesson.

19 1970s Politics and Fashion

> **Dear Parent or Teacher,**
>
> The Vietnam War was very controversial. Be aware of this if you do additional research or incorporate other material. Some protests were violent. Soldiers returning from the conflict were often treated shamefully by those who opposed the war.

Materials needed for this chapter:

- ✔ Student Activity Pages
- ✔ Pencil/eraser
- ✔ Colored pencils or crayons
- ✔ Globe and/or atlas
- ✔ Optional: Books or websites about fashion and cars of the 1970s

Oral Narration Questions and Answers

Q. Retell what you learned today about the Vietnam War.

A. Take time to discuss the Vietnam War, including the anti-war protests. Encourage your student to elaborate and make sure he or she can articulate how divisive the war was in America, and how this was different than previous wars.

Q. Talk about what you learned today about 1970s society.

A. Allow your student to narrate freely about what he or she learned in this chapter. Make sure the student can share some details about the fads, entertainment, and controversies of this time, as well as the struggle for Native American rights, and how religion was impacting American culture.

Optional Digging Deeper

- ✔ Your family may enjoy watching the movie *Woodlawn* (rated PG), which tells the story of a revival that sweeps through a troubled public school in the 1970s.

Written Narration Idea for Older Students:

Do you think America should have been involved in the Vietnam War? Why or why not?

_____

_____

_____

_____

_____

_____

_____

_____

SKETCHING

Name _____

1970s Politics and Fashion. The 1970s were a time of bright colors, bold fabrics, and tall shoes! You just got a job at a catalog company. It's time to sketch a new set of clothes on this catalog page — be sure to color it in afterwards!

1. Why do you think 1970s fashions were so extreme?

_____

_____

2. The Vietnam War was described as the first "television war." What does this mean?

_____

_____

_____

3. What were some of the protests by young Americans against the Vietnam War? What did other Americans think of these protests?

_____

_____

_____

4. Why did some people question President Nixon's commitment to ending the war?

_____

_____

_____

5. Who "won" the Vietnam War?

_____

_____

_____

6. Who is Reverend Billy Graham?

_____

_____

_____

MAP ADVENTURES

Name _____

970s Politics and Fashion. Here is a list of major cities that Reverend Billy Graham held
rusades in during the 1970s. Using a map or atlas for reference, find and mark the locations on the map
elow.

A. Baton Rouge	G. Dallas	M. Memphis	S. Phoenix
B. Birmingham	H. Kansas City	N. Milwaukee	T. Seattle
C. Charlotte	I. Knoxville	O. Minneapolis	U. South Bend
D. Chicago	J. Las Vegas	P. Nashville	V. St. Louis
E. Cincinnati	K. Lexington	Q. New York	W. Tampa
F. Cleveland	L. Los Angeles	R. Oakland	

. What were some of the fads and fashions people were enjoying in the 1970s?

_____

_____

_____

_____

2. What rights were American women fighting for in the 1970s?

_____

_____

_____

3. Native Americans were also actively protesting — why?

_____

_____

_____

Word Collectors:

4. Have you found the chapter's special word? Write it below:

   _____

Now, collect three other words you learned from this chapter by writing them below!

5. _____   6. _____   7. _____

Use each word in a separate sentence for your teacher.

Bonus! See if you can personalize your own VW camper van like the one on page 193 in the student book (top right). Draw the outline of the vehicle and then add your own personal designs and words.

1970s Politics and Fashion. Pretend that you are living in 1973 when the Vietnam War has just ended. Write a diary entry explaining your thoughts on the war. What were your opinions about it, the anti-war protests, and the draft?

_____

_____

_____

_____

_____

_____

_____

_____

_____

_____

_____

_____

_____

_____

_____

_____

_____

_____

_____

_____

_____

_____

My Timeline Manipulative. A timeline is a way to organize events of history in a logical, chronological way. If you would like to make this timeline element a part of a student's lesson, take some time to look over the important events of the current chapter. When creating their timeline, students can use sketches provided in the back of this Teacher Guide on pages 335–341. They may also choose to draw their own historical images or find them online. Use the timeline chart from the back and add information with each new lesson.

20 POLITICAL SCANDALS AND GASOLINE SHORTAGES

Materials needed for this chapter:

✔ Student Activity Pages

✔ Pencil/eraser

✔ Colored pencils or crayons

✔ Globe and/or atlas

Oral Narration Questions and Answers

Q. Talk about the Watergate scandal.

A. Make sure the student can talk about the break-in at the Watergate Hotel, the significance of the White House tapes, the result of the scandal (Nixon's resignation), and the effect it had of making people further distrust the government.

Q. Tell what you learned about the 1970s.

A. See what details your student shares with you about the decade. Make sure he or she understands the effect of the oil crisis and how unsure many people were of America's future.

Optional Digging Deeper

✔ From what foreign countries does the United States buy oil? Is there oil here in our country? If so, where? Do we sell it to other countries? You may wish to require your older student to look into these questions.

Written Narration Idea for Older Students:

Who was Spiro Agnew, and why was he removed as vice president?

_____

_____

_____

_____

_____

_____

_____

_____

SKETCHING

Name _____

Political Scandals and Gasoline Shortages. After Nixon's resignation, Gerald Ford became the president of the United States. Draw a picture of President Ford.

| **Angela's President Ford** | **My President Ford** |

1. What was so unusual about Gerald Ford's vice presidency and presidency?

_____

_____

_____

2. Why did Richard Nixon resign as president?

_____

_____

_____

3. What effect did the resignation and Watergate Scandal have on how Americans viewed the presidency?

_____

_____

_____

Copywork:

The President, Vice President, and all civil Officers of the United States shall be removed from Office on Impeachment for, and conviction of, Treason, Bribery, or other High Crimes and Misdemeanors.

—The Constitution

_____

_____

_____

_____

_____

What I am defending is the real rights of women.
A woman should have the right to be in the home as a wife and mother.

—Phyllis Schlafly

_____

_____

_____

_____

MAP ADVENTURES

Name _____

Political Scandals and Gasoline Shortages. Trace the pipeline's route through Alaska.
(See map in student book on page 201.)

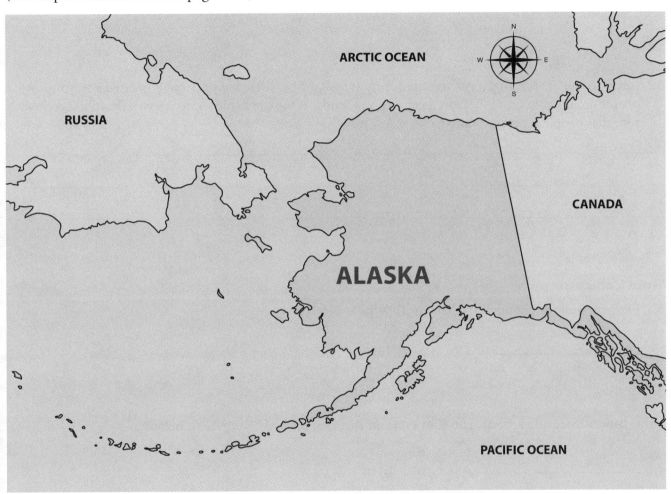

1. What event caused the Alaska pipeline to be approved?

_____

_____

_____

2. Why was it important to have a pipeline like this in the United States?

_____

_____

_____

3. What's the difference between an economic depression and an economic recession? Which one happened in the 1970s?

_____

_____

_____

4. Imagine you are running a gas station during the oil crisis. There is not enough gas to go around, and people are upset because they need gas to go to work. What are some strategies you could use to make sure that people are served fairly?

_____

_____

_____

Word Collectors:

5. Did you find the chapter's special word? Write it below:

   _____

Now, collect three other words you learned from this chapter by writing them below!

6. _____   7. _____   8. _____

Make sure you can explain the words to your teacher.

Political Scandals and Gasoline Shortages. Pretend that you are living during the oil crisis in 1973. You need gasoline for your car to go to work, but there are long lines at all the gas stations. Write a letter to your local Congressperson explaining your thoughts on the crisis. What effect is it having on Americans? What are some solutions to the problem?

_____

_____

_____

_____

_____

_____

_____

_____

_____

_____

_____

_____

_____

_____

_____

_____

_____

_____

_____

_____

My Timeline Manipulative. A timeline is a way to organize events of history in a logical, chronological way. If you would like to make this timeline element a part of a student's lesson, take some time to look over the important events of the current chapter. When creating their timeline, students can use sketches provided in the back of this Teacher Guide on pages 335–341. They may also choose to draw their own historical images or find them online. Use the timeline chart from the back and add information with each new lesson.

ARTIST STUDY

Name _____

Norman Rockwell (Illustrator). Norman Rockwell remains one of the best-known and most beloved American artists, even though when he was alive many art critics were dismissive of his work. He was born in 1894 in New York City and showed early talent. By the time he was a young man in the 1910s, he was already working as a magazine illustrator, a profession he continued until his death in 1978.

Rockwell became famous for his magazine covers and his illustrations for calendars. His charming, frequently humorous illustrations of everyday life, especially small-town life, were immediately popular with readers. Even without any accompanying text, Rockwell's illustrations told stories — and they were stories that the audience enjoyed.

Though he worked by commission and drew to meet the specifications and needs of the publications he worked for, his work always had a unique spin. His works were distinctive, featuring people with highly expressive faces, and showcased his excellent eye for detail. As a result, even as photography became more and more common in magazines, Rockwell's illustration work remained in demand.

The magazine Rockwell is most associated with is the *Saturday Evening Post*, though he also did a lot of work for *Look* and *Boys' Life* magazines and the Boy Scouts. Though critics claimed that Rockwell's work was overly nostalgic, he frequently focused on topical events. During World War II, his illustrations were used to urge Americans to buy war bonds. In the 1960s and 1970s, his work increasingly turned to the Civil Rights movement and poverty.

Examples of Illustrations by Norman Rockwell

Painting the Little House, 1921 (PD-Art)

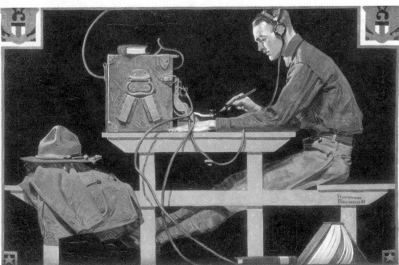

U.S. Army Teaches a Trade (G.I. Telegrapher) (PD-Art)

More Examples of Illustrations by Norman Rockwell

Freedom From Want (PD-US)

Saturday Evening Post cover, May 20, 1922.

Saturday Evening Post cover, Jan. 29, 1921.

Choose one of the following activities to understand more about Norman Rockwell's work.

1. You can either journal about or answer one or more of the following questions.

    ✔ Do you think it would be difficult to produce illustrations by commission for paying clients? Why or why not?

    ✔ Why do you think Rockwell's illustrations remained popular even after photography became popular?

    ✔ Many art critics were dismissive of Rockwell because they considered him an illustrator instead of an artist. Do you think that's a fair distinction to make? Do you consider illustration art?

2. Do an art assessment.

    ✔ What is the first thing you notice when you look at Rockwell's illustrations?

    ✔ Which of these illustrations is your favorite? Why?

    ✔ Rockwell was famous for his ability to tell an entire story with just one illustration. Pick one of the illustrations and describe what you think the story behind it is.

    ✔ Rockwell was also famous for the distinctive faces he drew. What do you notice about the people he drew? How are they different from the works of other artists you have seen?

3. Try it!

    ✔ You're going to try telling a story through images like Norman Rockwell! You won't be able to use panels to tell a sequence of events. Instead, you will have to decide the exact moment that perfectly tells the story. You might find it helpful to write the story out first. When you create your illustration, you can use paint like Rockwell or you can use colored pencils or crayons or whatever you like.

21 THE 1980s, PART ONE

Materials needed for this chapter:

✔ Student Activity Pages

✔ Pencil/eraser

✔ Colored pencils or crayons

✔ Globe and/or atlas

✔ Optional: Books about the 1980s and/or Ronald Reagan. Our family has enjoyed *Ronald Reagan, Young Leader* by Montrew Dunham.

Oral Narration Questions and Answers

Q. Talk about what you learned today about the 1980s.

A. Make sure the student understands that Ronald Reagan's approach to government and economics was very different than Jimmy Carter's.

Q. Retell what you learned about Reagan's presidency.

A. Be sure your student can talk about Reagan's second term and the farm crisis issue during his presidency.

Optional Digging Deeper

✔ Ronald Reagan was known as one of the great communicators of our country's history. I recommend that you take time to watch at least one speech by this president.

In the 1980s, an important movement was growing across the United States for parents to educate their children at home. Many moms chose to leave careers to commit to making sure their children had quality education opportunities that included values, and for some, Christian faith in their education. Some states had laws against homeschooling. See what you can learn about how homeschooling became prominent during this time and what laws protect parents who make the same choices to homeschool today. (Note: Home School Legal Defense Association - HSLDA is a good source for information on current laws.)

Written Narration Idea for Older Students:

What was "Reaganomics"? What effect did these policies have?

_____

_____

_____

_____

_____

_____

_____

_____

SKETCHING

Name _____

1980s, Part One. Draw Ronald Reagan.

1. What was the Iran Hostage Crisis?

_____

_____

_____

2. What is "mutually assured destruction" (MAD)?

_____

_____

_____

3. What were some of Reagan's policies as president?

_____

_____

_____

Copywork:

> **In this present crisis, government is not the solution to our problems;**
> **government is the problem.**
> **—Ronald Reagan**

_____

_____

_____

> **The greatest leader is not necessarily the one who does the greatest things.**
> **He is the one that gets the people to do the greatest things.**
> **—Ronald Reagan**

_____

_____

_____

_____

> **If we ever forget that we're one nation under God, then we will be one nation gone under.**
> **—Ronald Reagan**

_____

_____

_____

Day 128

MAP ADVENTURES

Name _____

1980s, Part One. Look at the maps on pages 210–211 of the student book. The first map shows the number of farms, and the second map shows the amount of farm land. (See map on pages 10–11 for state names.)

1. Which states show a significant decrease on both maps?

_____

_____

_____

_____

2. One thing to remember is that these maps are from the 2000s. What do you think might be different today compared to the 1980s for farmers?

_____

_____

_____

_____

3. What happened to the *Challenger* in 1986?

_____

_____

_____

_____

4. What did this remind Americans about the space program?

_____

_____

_____

_____

Word Collectors:

5. Did you find the chapter's special word? Write it below:

_____

Now, collect three other words you learned from this chapter by writing them below!

6. _____ 7. _____ 8. _____

Make sure you can explain the words to your teacher.

MY TIMELINE!

Name _____

1980s, Part One. Pretend that you have just learned about the *Challenger* explosion. What are your thoughts about it? Does the event change how you think of space travel? Write a diary entry to express your thoughts and feelings.

_____

_____

_____

_____

_____

_____

_____

_____

_____

_____

_____

_____

_____

_____

_____

_____

_____

_____

_____

_____

_____

_____

My Timeline Manipulative. A timeline is a way to organize events of history in a logical, chronological way. If you would like to make this timeline element a part of a student's lesson, take some time to look over the important events of the current chapter. When creating their timeline, students can use sketches provided in the back of this Teacher Guide on pages 335–341. They may also choose to draw their own historical images or find them online. Use the timeline chart from the back and add information with each new lesson.

22 THE 1980s, PART TWO

Materials needed for this chapter:

- ✔ Student Activity Pages
- ✔ Pencil/eraser
- ✔ Colored pencils or crayons
- ✔ Globe and/or atlas
- ✔ Optional: Books with pictures of the famous '80s big hair and magazines with '80s car ads. Please be warned, the movie ratings of the 1980s are extremely different than they are now. Movies, which seem safe because of a PG rating, may shock the viewer with swear words that would not be permitted in today's PG movies.

Oral Narration Questions and Answers

Q. Retell how the Cold War ended.

A. Make sure the student understands what the Cold War was and that it ended when several of the countries that were part of the Soviet Union left it.

Q. Talk about the three branches of government.

A. The student should be able to name the three branches and briefly summarize what each one does.

Optional Digging Deeper

- ✔ Do more research about the Berlin Wall. There is an extremely informative and interesting short video about the Berlin Wall on the History Channel™.

Written Narration Idea for Older Students:

Why was our government set up with a separation of powers?

_____

_____

_____

_____

_____

_____

_____

_____

SKETCHING

Name _____

1980s, Part Two. You are going to the Berlin Wall to join all of the people who are asking for it to be torn down. You plan on designing a T-shirt. What would you put on your T-shirt? Are there any words or pictures you want to add to the front and/or back?

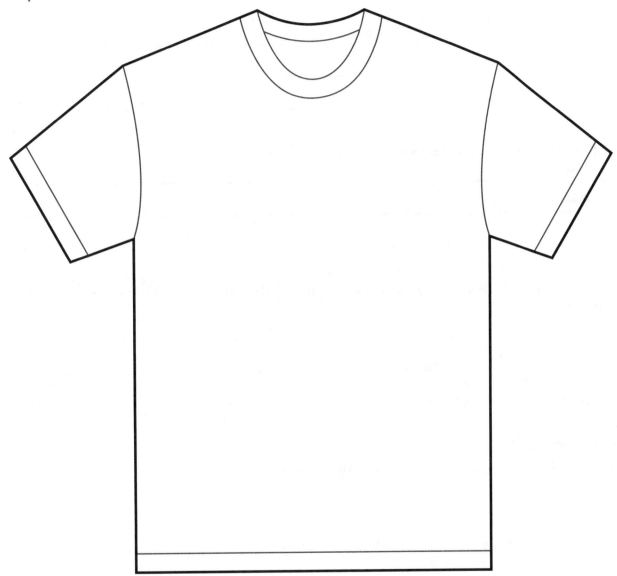

1. Pretend you are an American diplomat. You are going to negotiate with the East German government. What points are you going to use to argue in favor of tearing the wall down? Write out what you plan to say to them.

_____

_____

_____

_____

2. Describe the three branches of the United States government and what they do.

_____

_____

_____

_____

_____

_____

3. Explain how checks and balances work between the branches.

_____

_____

_____

4. Why do you think the Founding Fathers designed the government to work like this rather than letting one person do it all?

_____

_____

_____

Word Collectors:

5. Did you find the chapter's special word? Write it below:

_____

Now, collect three other words you learned from this chapter by writing them below!

6. _____   7. _____   8. _____

Make sure you can explain the words to your teacher.

Day 136

MAP ADVENTURES

Name _____

1980s, Part Two. You're going to be going on a trip to Washington, D.C.! You will have 5 days in the city. That's a lot of time, but there is also a lot to explore! You won't be able to see everything, so you will need to pick the 10 sites that you really want to make time for. These can be anything from government buildings to museums to memorials.

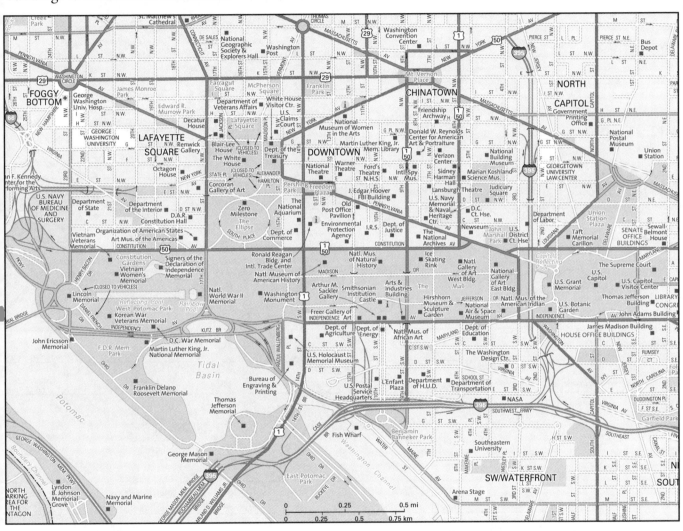

List the 10 sites that you want to see.

1. _____   6. _____

2. _____   7. _____

3. _____   8. _____

4. _____   9. _____

5. _____   10. _____

Now you need to figure out what you are going to do each day. Study your map — which sites are next to each other? It would be better to plan to see those things on the same day. You will also want to keep in mind how much time it takes to see a site. You probably won't spend as much time at a memorial as you would need for touring a museum or a government building, but you don't want to overschedule your day and rush through everything.

11. Day One:

_____

_____

_____

12. Day Two:

_____

_____

_____

13. Day Three:

_____

_____

_____

14. Day Four:

_____

_____

_____

15. Day Five:

_____

_____

_____

Now that you have planned your trip, go back to the map on the previous page and plan your route for each day!

MY TIMELINE!

Name _____

1980s, Part Two. Pretend that you are visiting Berlin when the Berlin Wall finally comes down. Your local newspaper has been in contact with you and would like you to describe what you saw. Write a letter to your local newspaper explaining what you witnessed and how it felt to be present.

_____

_____

_____

_____

_____

_____

_____

_____

_____

_____

_____

_____

_____

_____

_____

_____

_____

_____

_____

_____

My Timeline Manipulative. A timeline is a way to organize events of history in a logical, chronological way. If you would like to make this timeline element a part of a student's lesson, take some time to look over the important events of the current chapter. When creating their timeline, students can use sketches provided in the back of this Teacher Guide on pages 335–341. They may also choose to draw their own historical images or find them online. Use the timeline chart from the back and add information with each new lesson.

23 THE 1990S, PART ONE

Materials needed for this chapter:

- ✔ Student Activity Pages
- ✔ Pencil/eraser
- ✔ Colored pencils or crayons
- ✔ Globe and/or atlas

Oral Narration Questions and Answers

Q. Retell what you learned about computers.

A. Make sure your student understands that before the 1990s most people did not have access to a computer for personal use. During the 1990s, they became increasingly common.

Q. Talk about what you read about the Gulf War.

A. Make sure that your student understands the events that led up to the war and how it was resolved.

Optional Digging Deeper

- ✔ Find out how computers have changed over the years.

Written Narration Idea for Older Students:

How did the way people used computers become different in the 1990s?

_____

_____

_____

_____

_____

_____

_____

_____

SKETCHING

Name _____

The 1990s, Part One. Computer technology continues to change rapidly. Here's your chance to design your own computer! What extra features would you like to add? What shape would you like it to be? The choice is yours!

1. What are some of the design features you added to your computer? Why did you decide to include them?

_____

_____

_____

_____

2. Who was Saddam Hussein and what did he do to Kuwait?

_____

_____

_____

_____

3. How did America respond to Hussein's actions?

_____

_____

_____

_____

4. How was this war different from previous wars?

_____

_____

_____

_____

Copywork:

**True courage is being afraid, and going ahead
and doing your job anyhow, that's what courage is.
—General Norman Schwarzkopf**

_____

_____

_____

MAP ADVENTURES

Name _____

The 1990s, Part One. You work for an internet service provider. You have customers in town, but there are also people who live outside of town who want to be customers.

1. Where is the best place to locate a tower for people who both live in and outside of town? You can choose (A) the valley, (B) the foothills, or (C) the top of the mountain.

_____

_____

_____

_____

2. On the maps on pages 230–231 of the student book, there are a lot of places shown that still do not have internet service. Why is this?

_____

_____

_____

_____

_____

Word Collectors:

3. Did you find the chapter's special word? Write it below:

_____

Now, collect three other words you learned from this chapter by writing them below!

4. _____   5. _____   6. _____

Make sure you can explain the words to your teacher.

The 1990s, Part One. Pretend that the Persian Gulf War has just broken out. What is your opinion about the Iraqis invading Kuwait? What are your thoughts on American involvement in the war? Write a letter to a friend or relative explaining your feelings on the subject.

_____

_____

_____

_____

_____

_____

_____

_____

_____

_____

_____

_____

_____

_____

_____

_____

_____

_____

_____

My Timeline Manipulative. A timeline is a way to organize events of history in a logical, chronological way. If you would like to make this timeline element a part of a student's lesson, take some time to look over the important events of the current chapter. When creating their timeline, students can use sketches provided in the back of this Teacher Guide on pages 335–341. They may also choose to draw their own historical images or find them online. Use the timeline chart from the back and add information with each new lesson.

24 THE 1990S, PART TWO

Materials needed for this chapter:
- ✔ Student Activity Pages
- ✔ Pencil/eraser
- ✔ Colored pencils or crayons
- ✔ Globe and/or atlas
- ✔ Optional: Books or websites showing pictures taken by the Hubble Space Telescope

Oral Narration Questions and Answers

Q. Retell and discuss what you learned today about the 1990s.

A. Your student may talk about any topic that caught his or her attention, but make sure he or she understands the significance of impeachment and the meaning of political gridlock.

Q. Talk about what you read today about Y2K.

A. Make sure your student understands why people were frightened and the effect fear had on some people.

Optional Digging Deeper
- ✔ You may want your older student to investigate people's responses to the Y2K scare more in-depth.

Written Narration Idea for Older Students:

What happened with many of Bill Clinton's proposed laws when he was president? Why?

_____

_____

_____

_____

_____

_____

_____

_____

SKETCHING

Name _____

The 1990s, Part Two. Sketch your own picture of the Hubble Space Telescope!

1. What is the Hubble Space Telescope and why is it important?

_____

_____

_____

_____

2. What kind of government did Bill Clinton favor?

_____

_____

_____

_____

3. Why did the Y2K crisis make people so frightened?

_____

_____

_____

_____

MAP ADVENTURES

Name _____

The 1990s, Part Two. The Hubble Telescope orbits the earth and provides data to scientists. The data does not come directly from the telescope, though. The information is first transferred to a satellite in outer space before it goes to sites on the ground. From there, it goes to NASA's facilities in Maryland.

1. What challenges do you think it presents for NASA if they needed to send someone to the telescope to fix it?

_____
_____
_____
_____
_____
_____

2. Would it be easier to bring it back from space to repair or easier to send someone up to fix it in outer space?

_____
_____
_____
_____
_____
_____

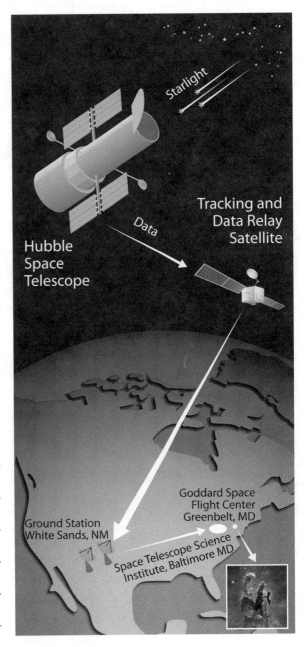

Word Collectors:

3. Did you find the chapter's special word? Write it below:

_____

Now, collect three other words you learned from this chapter by writing them below!

4. _____   5. _____   6. _____

Make sure you can explain the words to your teacher.

The 1990s, Part Two. Pretend that you are living in 1999, and everyone is preparing for Y2K. You've been put in charge of preparing for Y2K at your job. What is going through your mind? Are you concerned about it or do you think people are overreacting? What steps are you taking to prepare? Prepare notes on a speech you will give your coworkers.

_____

_____

_____

_____

_____

_____

_____

_____

_____

_____

_____

_____

_____

_____

_____

_____

_____

_____

_____

_____

_____

My Timeline Manipulative. A timeline is a way to organize events of history in a logical, chronological way. If you would like to make this timeline element a part of a student's lesson, take some time to look over the important events of the current chapter. When creating their timeline, students can use sketches provided in the back of this Teacher Guide on pages 335–341. They may also choose to draw their own historical images or find them online. Use the timeline chart from the back and add information with each new lesson.

25 THE STRANGE ELECTION OF 2000

Materials needed for this chapter:

✔ Student Activity Pages

✔ Pencil/eraser

✔ Colored pencils or crayons

✔ Globe and/or atlas

✔ Optional: Simple books or DVDs about the election process. I recommend the *Just the Facts: the Election Process in America* DVD.

Oral Narration Questions and Answers

Q. Retell what you learned about the electoral college.

A. Make sure the student understands how the electoral college works, and that it is what dictates who becomes president, not the popular vote.

Q. Talk about what happened in the 2000 election.

A. Make sure the student understands that Bush won because he won the electoral vote, despite not winning the popular vote. Also be sure that the student realizes the importance of Florida in this election.

Optional Digging Deeper

✔ You may want your older student to investigate the electoral college and the whole election process a little more in depth.

Written Narration Idea for Older Students:

Who would you have voted for in the 2000 election? Why?

_____

_____

_____

_____

_____

_____

_____

_____

SKETCHING

Name _____

The Strange Election of 2000. Voting is an important aspect of American life. When you go vote, you usually get a sticker that lets other people know that you participated! Draw a "VOTE" button like this one.

1. Thinking about the election of 2000, why is it important to vote?

_____

_____

_____

2. What do you think about the way each party goes about picking their candidates for president?

_____

_____

_____

3. Who were the candidates in the 2000 election?

_____

_____

_____

4. What made this election so strange?

_____

_____

_____

Word Collectors:

5. Did you find the chapter's special word? Write it below:

_____

Now, collect three other words you learned from this chapter by writing them below!

6. _____   7. _____   8. _____

Make sure you can explain the words to your teacher.

MAP ADVENTURES

Name _____

The Strange Election of 2000. The presidential election of 2000 was a very close race. Here is the electoral map for that year.

2000 ELECTORAL VOTE

List the 7 states that have more than 20 electoral votes.

1. _____   2. _____

3. _____   4. _____

5. _____   6. _____

7. _____

8. How many total electoral votes do these states have altogether? _____

Now, list the 7 states that have the lowest total of votes. (Hint: They all have 3; D.C. only has two and is not a state.)

9. _____

10. _____

11. _____

12. _____

13. _____

14. _____

15. _____

16. If you added them to the total number of electoral votes from the largest states, would you have enough to win the presidency? Why or why not?

_____

_____

_____

17. What is the minimum number of states that you would need to win the presidency through electoral votes? Be sure to explain your answer.

_____

_____

_____

18. Pretend you are running for president. You need to devise a strategy for your campaign. Based on what you know about the electoral college, which states do you plan to focus on?

_____

_____

_____

MY TIMELINE!

Name _____

The Strange Election of 2000. Why do you think the Founding Fathers of the United States chose to create the process for electing a president the way they did? Why not just have the candidate who won more votes overall be president?

_____

_____

_____

_____

_____

_____

_____

_____

_____

_____

_____

_____

_____

_____

_____

_____

_____

_____

_____

_____

_____

_____

_____

My Timeline Manipulative. A timeline is a way to organize events of history in a logical, chronological way. If you would like to make this timeline element a part of a student's lesson, take some time to look over the important events of the current chapter. When creating their timeline, students can use sketches provided in the back of this Teacher Guide on pages 335–341. They may also choose to draw their own historical images or find them online. Use the timeline chart from the back and add information with each new lesson.

ARTIST STUDY

Name _____

Dale Chihuly (Glass Artist). Born in 1941 in Washington State, Dale Chihuly initially studied interior design in college. He was introduced to glass art while a student and became fascinated with it. He ended up studying glasswork in Italy before returning to the United States to study it and sculpture.

Creating glasswork can be very tricky — the material is capable of being molded into various shapes but is also prone to breaking. It takes considerable practice and skill to sculpt it.

He was one of the early pioneers in teaching glass art. After suffering injuries in a series of accidents, he was unable to create on his own but worked through students and other artists to continue crafting his stunning glass sculptures. His work with a team of other artists has allowed him to create large-scale glass art. His glasswork has been displayed around the world and frequently uses eye-catching colors and designs.

Chihuly's work is often displayed in installations. Traditionally, people go to art galleries to look at works like paintings on a wall. Installations are 3-D art projects that have to be installed and are often designed to change how one views the space it occupies. Viewers can often walk around or under the installation.

Example of Glass Art by Dale Chihuly

Panoramio Exhibition. Attribution: Jiaqian AirplaneFan (CC BY 3.0)

More Examples of Glass Art by Dale Chihuly

Panoramio Exhibition. Attribution: Jiaqian AirplaneFan (CC BY 3.0)

Choose one of the following activities to understand more about Dale Chihuly's work.

1. You can either journal about or answer one or more of the following questions.

   ✔ Would you be interested in trying glasswork? Why or why not?

   ✔ Do you think installation art has a different effect on the viewer? Why or why not? Why do you think this form of art has become more popular over the years?

   ✔ If you were an artist, would you prefer to work alone or on a team? Why?

2. Do an art assessment.

   ✔ What is the first thing you notice when you look at Chihuly's installations?

   ✔ Which of these installations is your favorite? Why?

   ✔ Chihuly studied glass art extensively, but he also has a background in interior design and sculpture. How do you think that educational background is reflected in his glasswork?

   ✔ Chihuly cites architect Frank Lloyd Wright and abstract expressionist painters among his inspirations. How do you see their impact reflected in his work?

3. Try it!

   ✔ Glassblowing is fascinating and fun but can be dangerous without proper experience and equipment. With your parents' permission, research to see if there are any glassblowers or glass artists near where you live. They may hold demonstrations that allow you to watch them work, and some even hold classes.

26 "Evil, Despicable Acts of Terror"

Materials needed for this chapter:

- ✔ Student Activity Pages
- ✔ Pencil/eraser
- ✔ Colored pencils or crayons
- ✔ Globe and/or atlas
- ✔ Optional: See if you can find instances of patriotism following the attacks on September 11th. There were many news stories (local, state, and national), as well as television features, and special reports following the tragedy.

Oral Narration Questions and Answers

Q. Retell what happened on 9/11.

A. The student should understand that America was attacked by terrorists from al-Qaeda.

Q. Talk about what you read today about the 2000s.

A. Make sure your student can talk about the significance of the wars in Iraq and Afghanistan.

Optional Digging Deeper

- ✔ Find a video or recording of the speech that President George W. Bush gave about the attacks on September 20, 2001 to a joint session of Congress.

Written Narration Idea for Older Students:

How did the terrorist attacks on 9/11 bring America together?

_____

_____

_____

_____

_____

_____

_____

_____

SKETCHING

Name _____

"Evil, Despicable Acts of Terror." After the 9/11 terrorist attacks, Americans were eager to stand together and show their patriotism. It was a common sight to see American flags displayed. Sketch and color a flag in the space provided below.

1. What happened on 9/11?

_____

_____

_____

_____

_____

_____

_____

_____

_____

_____

2. What were some of America's responses to the attacks?

_____

_____

_____

_____

3. What were some of the security measures taken after 9/11?

_____

_____

_____

_____

4. What happened to Saddam Hussein?

_____

_____

_____

_____

MAP ADVENTURES

Name _____

"Evil, Despicable Acts of Terror." We learn in this chapter about the 9/11 terrorist attacks that resulted in the tragic loss of life of many. Sometimes natural disasters also create death, suffering, and hardship for Americans. Large portions of New Orleans were below sea level and relied on levees to hold that water back. During Katrina, these levees breached (were overflowed), and there was nothing to hold the floodwater back.

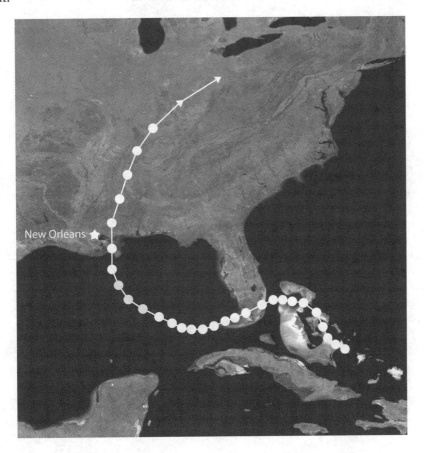

This map shows the expected storm track of Hurricane Katrina. Remember, the storm weakens the further it goes inland, and the arrow shows the path of the storm. You are a weather person who needs to start issuing warnings.

1. Which large city marked on the map is going to take a direct hit? _____

2. Which state is going to be affected in the beginning of the hurricane? _____

3. What do you think are some of the challenges involved with preparing a major city like New Orleans for a natural disaster?

_____

_____

_____

_____

_____

4. What are some possible solutions to the challenges of preparing a major city for a natural disaster?

_____

_____

_____

_____

_____

Word Collectors:

5. Did you find the chapter's special word? Write it below:

_____

Now, collect three other words you learned from this chapter by writing them below!

6. _____   7. _____   8. _____

Make sure you can explain the words to your teacher.

"Evil, Despicable Acts of Terror." Pretend that the war in Afghanistan has just started, shortly after the 9/11 terrorist attacks. What are your thoughts and feelings about this war? Write a letter to a relative or friend explaining your own ideas about the war.

_____

_____

_____

_____

_____

_____

_____

_____

_____

_____

_____

_____

_____

_____

_____

_____

_____

_____

_____

_____

My Timeline Manipulative. A timeline is a way to organize events of history in a logical, chronological way. If you would like to make this timeline element a part of a student's lesson, take some time to look over the important events of the current chapter. When creating their timeline, students can use sketches provided in the back of this Teacher Guide on pages 335–341. They may also choose to draw their own historical images or find them online. Use the timeline chart from the back and add information with each new lesson.

27 MORE RECENT HISTORY

Materials needed for this chapter:

✔ Student Activity Pages

✔ Pencil/eraser

✔ Colored pencils or crayons

✔ Globe and/or atlas

Oral Narration Questions and Answers

Q. Discuss what you read about Presidents Bush and Obama.

A. Make sure your student can talk about events that occurred in each presidency.

Q. Retell and discuss what we have read so far today.

A. Be sure your student can discuss the presidential election of 2016, including the candidates.

Optional Digging Deeper

✔ Research presidential inauguration traditions. If your student has a favorite president, let him or her do some research to learn more about that president's inauguration(s).

Written Narration Idea for Older Students:

What were some of the key issues in the 2016 election?

_____

_____

_____

_____

_____

_____

_____

_____

SKETCHING

Name _____

More Recent History. In 2016, Donald Trump was elected 45th president of the United States. Every president needs an official portrait. Draw him.

1. What were some of the difficulties that George W. Bush faced during his second term?

_____

_____

_____

2. Why was the housing market having such difficulties in 2008?

_____

_____

_____

_____

_____

3. What did Barack Obama promise voters when he ran for president?

_____

_____

_____

_____

_____

4. How was President Obama's Affordable Care Act an example of big government?

_____

_____

_____

_____

_____

MAP ADVENTURES

Name _____

More Recent History. Americans of all ages were excited by the solar eclipse in August 2017. Look at the map and answer the following questions.

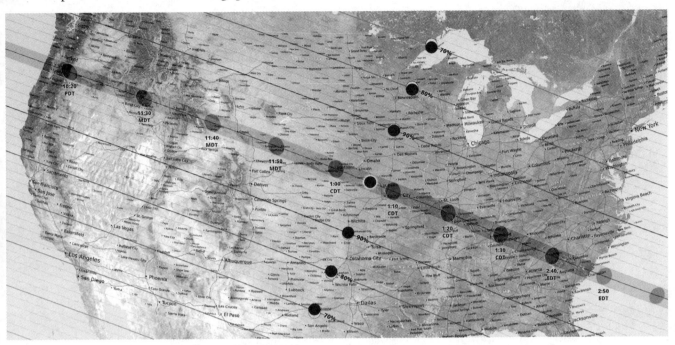

1. What sort of eclipse did people in your town see? Look at the map and see if your town is in the path of totality. If not, check to see what percentage of the eclipse was visible.

_____

_____

_____

2. What's the biggest city near you that was in the path of totality? _____

3. How far would you need to travel to have been in the path of totality? Would you have had to drive for days or was it visible from your own home?

_____

_____

_____

Word Collectors:

4. Did you find the chapter's special word? Write it below:

_____

Now, collect three other words you learned from this chapter by writing them below!

5. _____   6. _____   7. _____

Make sure you can explain the words to your teacher.

More Recent History. Pretend that you are part of a missions trip to help people in New Orleans and on the Gulf Coast after Hurricane Katrina. What are the conditions like? What have you seen? How is your group helping them? Write a letter to your local newspaper explaining what is going on.

_____

_____

_____

_____

_____

_____

_____

_____

_____

_____

_____

_____

_____

_____

_____

_____

_____

_____

_____

_____

_____

_____

My Timeline Manipulative. A timeline is a way to organize events of history in a logical, chronological way. If you would like to make this timeline element a part of a student's lesson, take some time to look over the important events of the current chapter. When creating their timeline, students can use sketches provided in the back of this Teacher Guide on pages 335–341. They may also choose to draw their own historical images or find them online. Use the timeline chart from the back and add information with each new lesson.

28 PROTECTORS OF OUR FREEDOM

Materials needed for this chapter:

- ✔ Student Activity Pages
- ✔ Pencil/eraser
- ✔ Colored pencils or crayons
- ✔ Globe and/or atlas
- ✔ Optional: Books or websites about the different branches of the armed services

Oral Narration Questions and Answers

Q. Retell what you learned about the military.

A. The student should be able to briefly describe the differences between the Army and the Marines.

Q. Talk about what you learned about our armed forces.

A. Make sure the student can discuss the differences between the Navy, the Air Force, and the Coast Guard.

Optional Digging Deeper

- ✔ This would be a wonderful time to discover more about our nation's military cemeteries and military funeral traditions. Your student might also enjoy sending a thank you card to a veteran he or she knows personally.

Written Narration Idea for Older Students:

Which branch of the military do you find the most interesting? Why?

_____

_____

_____

_____

_____

_____

_____

_____

SKETCHING

Name _____

Protectors of Our Freedom. Draw an eagle.

1. The eagle is a common emblem for our country and its military forces. What is it about eagles that might inspire people?

_____

_____

_____

2. Briefly describe what each military branch does.

_____

_____

_____

_____

_____

_____

_____

3. Why do you think each military branch has its own unique job?

_____

_____

_____

_____

4. Even though the military branches are different from each other, they also must work together. What are some ways that they do that?

_____

_____

_____

_____

MAP ADVENTURES

Name _____

Protectors of Our Freedom. This map shows where the service academies are located.

1. Why do you think so many of the service academies would be near Washington, D.C.?

_____

_____

_____

2. Why do you think the entrance requirements for the service academies are so difficult?

_____

_____

_____

3. We need to remember to always honor and respect veterans. What are some ways that you can do this?

_____

_____

_____

_____

_____

_____

_____

_____

_____

_____

_____

_____

Word Collectors:

4. Did you find the chapter's special word? Write it below:

_____

Now, collect three other words you learned from this chapter by writing them below!

5. _____ 6. _____ 7. _____

Make sure you can explain the words to your teacher.

MY TIMELINE!

Name _____

Protectors of Our Freedom. Pretend that it is November 2016, and Donald Trump has just been elected the 45th president. What is the most important issue that you think the country is facing? What are some solutions to this problem? Write a letter to the president to discuss your ideas.

_____

_____

_____

_____

_____

_____

_____

_____

_____

_____

_____

_____

_____

_____

_____

_____

_____

_____

_____

_____

_____

My Timeline Manipulative. A timeline is a way to organize events of history in a logical, chronological way. If you would like to make this timeline element a part of a student's lesson, take some time to look over the important events of the current chapter. When creating their timeline, students can use sketches provided in the back of this Teacher Guide on pages 335–341. They may also choose to draw their own historical images or find them online. Use the timeline chart from the back and add information with each new lesson.

ARTIST STUDY

Name _____

Maya Lin (Memorial Designer). The daughter of Chinese immigrants, Lin was born in 1959 in Ohio. She was a 21-year-old architecture student at Yale when a competition to create a memorial for the Vietnam War was announced. Professional architects and architecture students were invited to enter and told that the monument needed to avoid the still-controversial politics surrounding the war and include the names of all American service members who died during it. One of Lin's teachers made the contest part of the coursework for their class for the semester.

Most people in her class and others who entered the competition envisioned some literal monument, such as sculptures of eagles or combat boots or military helmets or soldiers in action. To fit in with other monuments in Washington, D.C., most of the proposals featured white monuments. Lin, however, envisioned a black V-shaped wall with the names of the over 50,000 Americans who died in the war, listed in chronological order.

She won the competition due to the stark simplicity of her monument design, but controversy soon erupted. Some criticized the abstractness of the design while others criticized the color. Still others were unhappy she was not yet a professional architect while others accused her of being too young to understand the war and a few even insultingly questioned whether the design should come from someone of Asian heritage.

(CC BY-SA 3.0)

Lin, however, was adamant that the focus should not be on her but on the memorial and that the design elements would force visitors to focus on the people who fought in the war. She also maintained that the memorial needed to be polished black marble so that people viewing the memorial would see their own reflections in it. Despite the initial controversy, people were overwhelmingly supportive of the memorial after it was built, with many thinking it is the most emotionally affecting monument in Washington, D.C. To this day, millions of people visit the memorial every year.

Civil Rights Memorial in Montgomery, Alabama, Markuskun (PD-US).

Lin is still best known for her work on the Vietnam Veterans Memorial, but she has also designed several other notable monuments, including the Civil Rights Memorial in Montgomery, Alabama.

Vietnam Veterans Memorial in Washington, D.C.

Copying a name at the Vietnam Vets Memorial

Choose one of the following activities to understand more about Maya Lin's work.

1. You can either journal about or answer one or more of the following questions.

    ✓ Why do you think it was a requirement that the Vietnam Memorial include the names of the soldiers who were killed in the war?

    ✓ Why do you think it was so important to Lin that visitors' faces be reflected back at them when they viewed the Vietnam Memorial?

    ✓ Lin has said that she based her Civil Rights Memorial design on the concept of water and that she intends it to be soothing. What design elements reflect this intention?

2. Do an art assessment.

    ✓ What is the first thing you notice when you look at the Vietnam Memorial?

    ✓ How does the design affect your emotions when you are viewing it? Do you think that it would be different in person? Why or why not?

    ✓ Lin has said that the monument requires people to think about the people, not the politics of the war. What design elements do this? Why?

    ✓ What similarities do you see between the Vietnam and the Civil Rights memorials? What differences?

3. Try it!

    ✓ Many towns have monuments — there's a good chance that your town does. Pay it a visit or find pictures of it. What are its design elements? What effect do you think the designer intended it to have on visitors? Does the design help achieve this effect? How so? If you were going to design a memorial for your town, what design elements would you include?

My Book of Service

"My little children, let us not love [only] in word, neither in tongue; but in deed and in truth." —1 John 3:18

Service Scriptures:

- 1 John 3:18
- Galatians 5:13–14
- Mark 10:44–45
- Proverbs 19:17
- Proverbs 14:21
- Matthew 25:35–40
- Ephesians 2:10
- Hebrews 6:10–12

Assembly instructions:

Cut out the booklet pages on the following Journal pages (265–268). Line them up and staple them together. Each week, you will write about what act of service you have chosen to do. Below are some ideas to get you started. (Look online with your teacher for organizations that specialize in these activities.)

- Gather toys or pack food for an organization.
- Write letters to soldiers who are on active duty.
- Work at a food shelf or pantry.
- Go through toys and clothes — take outgrown items to a store that helps people during rough times.
- Serve a meal at a soup kitchen.
- Make a meal for a neighbor and deliver it with a nice card or note.
- Find a missionary to write and encourage.
- If your family can afford it, start sponsoring a needy child in a foreign country.
- Your idea:_____
- Your idea:_____

My Book
of Service

Name _____

Take my life and let it be
Consecrated, Lord, to Thee.
Take my moments and my days;
Let them flow in ceaseless praise.
Take my hands, and let them move
At the impulse of Thy love.
Take my feet, and let them be
Swift and 'beautiful' for Thee.
Take my voice, and let me sing,
Always, only, for my King.
Take my lips, and let them be
Filled with messages from Thee.
Take my silver and my gold;
Not a mite would I withhold.
Take my intellect, and use
Every power as Thou shalt choose.
Take my will and make it Thine,
It shall be no longer mine.
Take my heart, it is Thine own,
It shall be Thy royal throne.
Take my love; my Lord, I pour
At Thy feet its treasure-store.
Take myself, and I will be
Ever, only, ALL for Thee.
by Frances R. Havergal*

*Frances Ridley Havergal, *Kept for the Master's Use*
(London: James Nisbet & Co., 1883), 6.

Week 22:

_____

_____

Week 23:

_____

_____

Week 24:

_____

_____

Week 25:

_____

_____

Week 26:

_____

_____

Week 27:

_____

_____

Week 28:

_____

_____

4

Week 1:

_____

_____

Week 2:

_____

_____

Week 3:

_____

_____

Week 4:

_____

_____

Week 5:

_____

_____

Week 6:

_____

_____

Week 7:

_____

_____

1

Week 8:

_____

_____

Week 9:

_____

_____

Week 10:

_____

_____

Week 11:

_____

_____

Week 12:

_____

_____

Week 13:

_____

_____

Week 14:

_____

_____

She opens her mouth with wisdom,
And on her tongue is the law
of kindness (Proverbs 31:26).

2

Week 15:

_____

_____

Week 16:

_____

_____

Week 17:

_____

_____

Week 18:

_____

_____

Week 19:

_____

_____

Week 20:

_____

_____

Week 21:

_____

_____

… put on tender mercies, kindness, humility,
meekness, longsuffering; bearing with one
another, and forgiving one another, if anyone has a
complaint against another; even as Christ forgave
you, so you also must do (Colossians 3:12–13).

3

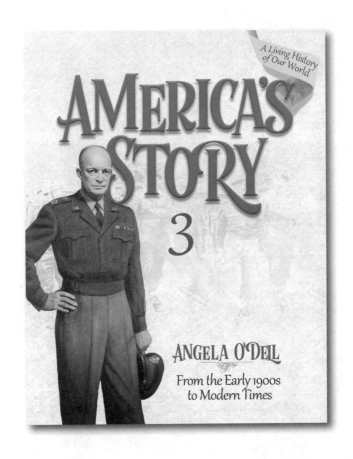

A Living History of Our World

AMERICA'S STORY
3

ANGELA O'DELL

From the Early 1900s
to Modern Times

Review Sheets

for Use with

America's Story 3

REVIEW SHEET I

Name _____

Find the names of the people, places, things, and events you have learned about this year!

```
D Z Z A J B U L L M O O S E P A R T Y E
A F O O D A D M I N I S T R A T I O N N
K O D I L X N O P N R T A O B E F I L I
O R M B S C O P E S T R I A L I H I W M
T D R O F Y R N E H S E S A I C T N O C
A M S R T L T A O A C N C I A E C O R O
T O A V N U H I S T C I R M G B L S L N
E T U I O L A S N L N H G O Y E A L D V
R O R L I F T B E A H N R D L R N I W E
R R S L T H L D T O I G T E I G A W A Y
I C S E I S A I R Y E X C L T S C W R O
T O K W B I T P L S E L P T A C A O O R
O M I R I N I F L A P P E R Y B M R N T
R P R I H A C D I M B F T N R C A D E R
Y A E G O P O H F Z A R C S A E N O O E
S N G H R S C H E F A M I L Y L A O E N
D Y O T P T E E B E S P R O C E P W H C
K I T T Y H A W K N O R T P A C E R T H
W S I N K I N G T H G I R W R U B L I W
R E D S U M M E R E N Y M E S L Y B S A
```

1. Airplane
2. Bull Moose Party
3. Conveyor
4. Dakota Territory
5. Flapper
6. Flying Machine
7. Food Administration
8. Ford Motor Company
9. Henry Ford
10. Iceberg
11. Jazz
12. Kitty Hawk
13. Lifeboat
14. Model T
15. North Atlantic Ocean
16. Orville Wright
17. Panama Canal
18. Prohibition
19. Red Summer
20. Scopes Trial
21. Sinking
22. Spanish Flu
23. Titanic
24. Trench
25. Wilbur Wright
26. Woodrow Wilson
27. World War One

REVIEW SHEET II

Part I

Name _____

Unscramble the Answer:

1. U.S. President after Harding dies: **Civlan oCdiloge**

   _____

2. U.S. area suffering dust storms: **Dsut Bwol**

   _____

3. President who served more terms than any other: **Frlknain D Roevesolt**

   _____

4. Period of economic devastation during the late 1920s and 1930s: **Gaert Depsserion**

   _____

5. Unpopular president at the end of the 1920s: **beeHrrt Hevoor**

   _____

6. What you do when you buy stocks: **Invtse**

   _____

7. FDR's plan for economic recovery: **Nwe Dael**

   _____

8. The source of the Great Crash on Black Tuesday: **Scotk Mekrat**

   _____

9. Tells you the current price of stocks and bonds: **Tekcir tpae**

   _____

10. The state of being without a job: **nUemyolpmtne**

    _____

REVIEW SHEET II

Part II

Name _____

World War II Crossword Challenge: Turn the page on its side and use the following clues to fill in the crossword puzzle with the names of important people, places, and events in American history!

Across

1. Sunken ship and site of memorial
3. Target of the Dec. 7, 1941 sneak attack
5. Advance military force who jumped from planes
6. Led a daring bombing raid against Japan
8. Items purchased during World War II to help with wartime costs
11. Military strategy to get close enough to attack Japan
14. Advocated by African American veterans to end segregation
17. American general who famously returned to Philippines
18. Country whose forces attacked Pearl Harbor
19. One of several island chains that were "hopped"
20. Ultimate goal of United States for World War II
21. Target of the first atomic bomb in Japan

Down

2. American soldiers who served in segregated units
4. Turning point for U.S. forces in the Pacific Theater
7. Nickname of B-17 bombers in World War II
9. Weapons dropped on Japanese cities of Hiroshima and Nagasaki
10. Places where Japanese Americans were forced to relocate to
12. U.S. holding occupied by Japanese forces in World War II
13. European country led by Adolf Hitler
15. Native Americans who worked to keep communication secure
16. America during World War II

Mix and Match! (match the letter to the appropriate description)

1. _____ Effort to hold Nazi Germany accountable for atrocities
2. _____ U.S. effort to rebuild war-damaged countries after WWII
3. _____ Divided country at the heart of a proxy between U.S. and Soviet Union
4. _____ Effort to bring food and supplies to blockaded Berlin by U.S. planes
5. _____ President who approved the use of atomic weapons against Japan
6. _____ Former general who became president after WWII
7. _____ Communist group of countries following the Russian Revolution
8. _____ State of conflict between the U.S. and the Soviet Union
9. _____ Place prepared with food and supplies to protect against radiation and fallout

a) Berlin Airlift
b) Cold War
c) Dwight Eisenhower
d) Fallout Shelter
e) Harry S. Truman

f) Korea
g) Marshall Plan
h) Nuremberg Trials
i) Soviet Union

REVIEW SHEET III

Name _____

1950s – Who's Who and What's What?

1. Famous highway between Chicago, IL and Los Angeles, CA. _____

2. Singer followed by screaming fans. _____

3. Television show popular in the 1950s. _____

4. Popular skirt in the 1950s. _____

5. A person who supports an idea or organization. _____

6. U.S. Senator known for trying to find communists. _____

7. Someone not allowed to work because of accusations. _____

8. This led to separate drinking fountains and other things. _____

Timeline Twisters!

Match each event with the year it happened.

1. Cuban Missile Crisis. _____		1952
2. John Kennedy elected president. _____		1953
3. Korean War Armistice. _____		1954
4. Dwight Eisenhower elected president. _____		1960
5. Dr. King's assassination. _____		1962
6. Neil Armstrong walks on the moon. _____		1962
7. Desegregation of U.S. schools. _____		1964
8. Montgomery bus boycott. _____		1968
9. Freedom Summer in Mississippi. _____		1969
10. Occupation of Alcatraz Island ends. _____		1971
11. Nixon re-elected. _____		1972
12. U.S. ends Vietnam War. _____		1973
13. Ford becomes president. _____		1974
14. Carter elected president. _____		1976
15. Reagan elected president. _____		1980

Word Search:

```
S  A  T  A  I  R  A  T  E  R  C  E  S  T  A  R  W  A  R  S
U  I  P  E  Z  E  O  I  S  A  E  K  P  A  I  O  Y  L  M  N
P  S  D  I  L  X  C  O  P  G  R  X  A  S  R  S  J  R  O  I
R  Y  M  B  P  B  P  O  I  A  I  S  W  T  D  N  E  I  J  M
E  R  M  O  T  E  L  R  P  L  S  P  S  A  I  V  T  C  O  P
M  E  S  C  T  L  L  A  O  A  C  A  F  R  H  A  C  H  W  E
E  M  A  G  O  T  S  I  S  T  C  R  D  O  G  O  X  A  A  A
C  O  U  G  I  O  O  S  N  L  E  L  I  E  Y  M  O  L  T  C
O  G  R  F  R  P  I  B  E  E  A  S  R  S  L  A  Z  L  E  H
U  T  S  G  O  N  F  D  L  Z  T  G  T  O  I  V  B  E  R  M
R  N  S  N  A  C  I  O  Z  L  E  X  C  S  T  S  B  N  G  E
T  O  K  T  K  F  S  U  Y  S  E  L  P  E  A  C  E  G  A  N
J  M  I  I  V  D  B  I  E  A  A  B  M  G  Y  B  N  E  T  T
W  O  R  C  M  I  J  D  D  M  B  F  T  F  R  C  F  R  E  Q
N  Z  E  I  P  P  I  H  E  Z  A  R  C  S  S  E  N  T  I  F
S  E  G  A  T  S  O  H  C  F  A  M  I  L  Y  F  A  R  M  S
D  R  O  F  Y  T  T  E  B  E  S  P  R  O  C  E  A  E  P
K  S  E  G  R  E  G  A  T  I  O  N  S  P  A  C  E  L  A  B
W  Q  Q  U  R  C  I  V  I  L  R  I  G  H  T  S  T  M  U  W
R  Z  Z  B  I  L  L  Y  G  R  A  H  A  M  Q  T  F  A  R  D
```

1. Apollo
2. Assassination
3. Bay of Pigs
4. Bell Bottoms
5. Betty Ford
6. Billy Graham
7. Buzz Aldrin
8. Challenger
9. Civil Rights
10. Desegregation
11. Disco
12. Draft
13. Family Farms
14. Fidel Castro
15. Fitness Craze
16. Hippie
17. Hostages
18. Impeachment
19. Jim Crow
20. Malcolm X
21. Montgomery
22. Oil Crisis
23. Peace
24. Peace Corps
25. Pipeline
26. Protests
27. Rosa Parks
28. Secretariat
29. Segregation
30. Space Lab
31. Star Wars
32. Supreme Court
33. Watergate

REVIEW SHEET IV

Name _____

Do You Know Me?

1. I played a big part in ending the Cold War with the Soviet Union. _____

2. I was a barrier that divided a large city in Germany. _____

3. I became president in 1989. _____

4. I led American forces in the Gulf War. _____

5. I was elected president twice and faced impeachment. _____

6. I am a space telescope that can see distant stars and galaxies. _____

7. I lost the presidential election in the year 2000. _____

8. I won the presidential election of 2000. _____

9. I was the target in New York of terrorists on 9/11. _____

10. I was America's first African American president. _____

Monumental!

Label the images below with the name of each monument.

1. _____   2. _____   3. _____   4. _____

5. _____   6. _____   7. _____   8. _____

Which is which?

Match the branch of government with its components; mark it with **L** for legislative, **E** for executive, **J** for judicial.

_____Federal Courts

_____Cabinet

_____House of Representatives

_____President

_____Congress

_____Supreme Court

_____Senate

_____Vice President

FINAL REVIEW SHEET

Name _____

Part I

It's Presidential: match the policies and the president!

Barack Obama	Franklin D. Roosevelt	Harry S. Truman	Richard Nixon
Calvin Coolidge	George H.W. Bush	Herbert Hoover	Ronald Reagan
Donald Trump	George W. Bush	Jimmy Carter	Theodore Roosevelt
Dwight D. Eisenhower	Gerald Ford	Lyndon B. Johnson	Woodrow Wilson

1. The former vice-president-turned-president who chose to increase American troop levels in Vietnam by 1965.
   _____

2. A break-in and scandal led this president to resign from office. _____

3. This American became the 38th president of the United States without ever running for office.
   _____

4. This candidate became president following the strange election of 2000 and because of 9/11, created the Department of Homeland Security. _____

5. This president was the first African American to hold the office and signed legislation requiring all Americans to have health insurance. _____

6. His opponent was a former senator, first lady, and Secretary of State, but this businessman with no political experience became the 45th president of the United States.
   _____

7. A president with a "bigger government" view who created the Department of Education and Department of Energy. _____

8. A former actor turned president who promoted smaller government and had an economic program named after him. _____

9. This 41st president had to confront dictators on the other side of the world in the Persian Gulf.
   _____

10. Won re-election to the presidency with the slogan "He kept us out of war." _____

11. Became president after Warren Harding died. _____

12. President who refused policies that gave aid directly to citizens during the Great Depression.
    _____

13. This new president offered a hurting country a "New Deal" with CCC jobs and training programs.
    _____

14. Approved the use of a top-secret weapon to end the war with Japan. _____

15. Former WWII general who promised an end to the war in Korea and approved an armistice.
    _____

16. Encouraged laws to make meat and other food industries safer. _____

War – Around the World!

Write in the name of the war America participated in based on the description. (Some answers will be repeated.)

1. This war helped to spread the Spanish flu. _____

2. Americans fought in Cuba during this war. _____

3. Troops fought hard on the sands of Iwo Jima in this war. _____

4. The U.S. Army fought in the trenches of Europe in this war. _____

5. Dictator Saddam Hussein was a target of this war. _____

6. This proxy war left a country still divided today. _____

7. America claimed the Philippines after winning this war. _____

8. This war created protests and opposition to the draft. _____

9. D-Day was a significant event in this war. _____

10. Reparations after this war made the world's economy worse. _____

Quotable! Identify the person associated with the quote.

1. We need not seek courage outside of our history. _____

2. Politics make me sick. _____

3. Ask not what your country can do for you; ask what you can do for your country.

   _____

4. Yesterday, December 7, 1941 — a date which will live in infamy — the United States of America was suddenly and deliberately attacked by naval and air forces of the Empire of Japan.

   _____

5. With God in charge, I believe everything will work out for the best in the end. So what is there to worry about? _____

FINAL REVIEW SHEET
Part II

Name _____

Trial of the Century!

1. Dayton, TN was the site of what famous trial in 1925? _____

2. What was the focus of the trial? _____

3. Who was the prosecutor? _____

4. Who was John T. Scopes' lawyer? _____

Newsmakers!

1. Theodore Roosevelt created the _____ party.

2. The unsinkable ship that sank on its first voyage. _____

3. This inventor not only made a better car, but developed better manufacturing of it.

   _____

4. These brothers studied birds to make a machine to let men fly. _____

5. American passengers were killed when German U-boats targeted this ship. _____

6. This outbreak killed millions in the early 1900s. _____

7. The era when alcohol was prohibited. _____

8. The outcome of this trial in 1925 is still seen in schools today. _____

9. The Red Summer of 1919 was caused by what two things? _____

10. The events of Black Tuesday affected what economic center? _____

11. During this time, life in America was hard; people were jobless and homeless. _____

12. The "day that will live in infamy" referenced attacks at what place? _____

13. These Americans had to live in special camps in the U.S. during WWII. _____

14. Island-hopping was a WWII strategy to reach which country? _____

15. D-Day was a massive Allied invasion of what continent? _____

16. These trials forced the world to see the extent of Nazi atrocities. _____

17. Segregation and Jim Crow laws targeted what group of Americans? _____

18. This was a war that went on for decades between the Soviet Union and America. _____

19. What weapons technology used at the end of WWII frightened people? _____

20. What was the decade of American history known as the "Golden Age of America"? _____

21. This movement for equality involved bus boycotts, marches, and school integration. _____

22. This was perhaps the scariest event of the Cold War in 1962. _____

23. The Soviet Union won the space race, but what country reached the moon first? _____

24. Supreme Court decisions in the early 1960s targeted what issues in public schools? _____

25. This African American leader gave the famous "I Have a Dream" speech.

_____

26. She refused to sit at the back of the bus and was arrested. _____

27. This evangelist led massive crusades in the 1970s in America. _____

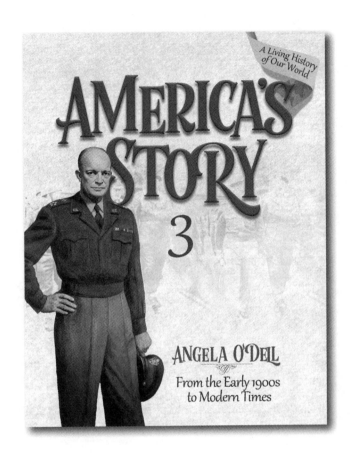

Answer Keys

for Use with

America's Story 3

Page 22

Answers may vary; however, student should consider his appreciation for wildlife at a young age (p. 6) and his adventures in the Dakotas as an adult (p. 7).

Page 23

1. Young Teddy Roosevelt started his very own museum to show off the creatures he had caught, killed (or found dead), and studied. The "Roosevelt Museum of Natural History" was housed in the Roosevelts' basement. (p. 6)

Page 24

2. The deaths of his wife and his mother. (p. 7)

Page 25

1. Western
2. Nevada and Utah
3. Bureau of Indian Affairs
4. Forest Service
5. Fish and Wildlife Service

Page 26

6. POLITICAL MACHINE (p. 8)
7. Answers may vary.
8. Answers may vary.
9. Answer may vary.
10. Answers may vary.
11. Answers may vary.
12. Answers may vary.
13. President
14. Police Commissioner
15. Author
16. Deputy Sherriff
17. Assemblyman

Page 27

Answers may vary.

Page 30

Answers may vary; however, student should show an understanding of the following text:

There has always been a fight to balance government for the people and by the people. In the year 1900, there were many issues that needed to be addressed, such as child labor, the lack of labor laws, and large company monopolies. The goal of the Progressive Movement was to use the government at every level to institute needed reforms. This idea minimizes the intellect and ingenuity of the individual citizen to come up with ways to solve problems. (p. 16)

Page 31

1. This amazing canal allowed ships to pass through Central America, connecting the Pacific Ocean to the Atlantic Ocean. This meant faster ship travel for those ships that used to have to travel all the way down to the tip of South America, or through the Strait of Magellan or Cape Horn. (p. 17)

2. The goal of the Progressive Movement was to use the government at every level to institute needed reforms. This idea minimizes the intellect and ingenuity of the individual citizen to come up with ways to solve problems. (p. 16)

Page 32

3. To preserve, protect and defend the Constitution of the United States to the best of the president's ability.

Page 33

1. As a child, Woodrow Wilson struggled with reading (he may have had dyslexia) and suffered from frail health. (p. 19)

Page 34

2. The "Bull Moose" party effectively split the Republican Party. This split allowed the Democratic nominee to win the presidency by a landslide. (p. 18)

3. Roosevelt (p. 18)
4. Taft (p. 18)
5. Wilson (p. 19)
6. Roosevelt (p. 17)

7. Taft (p. 18)

8. Wilson (p. 19)

9. MONOPOLY (p. 19)

10. Answers may vary.

11. Answers may vary.

12. Answers may vary.

Page 35

Answers may vary; however, student should show an understanding of the difficult task at hand, and the potential risk of disease, as discussed on page 20 of the student book.

Page 38

Answers may vary.

Page 39

1. The boys became interested in flying when their father brought home a toy helicopter. It was a flimsy little copy of a French invention, but the boys loved the toy so much that they made another one when the original broke. (p. 26)

Page 40

2. Answers may vary; but may include: The brothers designed and built their own printing press; the brothers opened their own bicycle repair shop in 1892, and began making their own brand of bikes in 1896; the brothers invented the first flying machines which served as a starting point for the planes we have today.

3. They used the money from their bicycle repair shop to pay for their new hobby and interest — flying! (p. 26)

4. Answers may vary.

Page 42

1. Answers may vary; however, answers should reflect the images given of pages 32–33 in the student book.

2. GLIDER (p. 28)

3. Answers may vary.

4. Answers may vary.

5. Answers may vary.

Page 43

Answers may vary; however, student should understand the excitement that would have taken place on account of this massive feat for America — and even the world.

Page 46

Henry had not been satisfied with the quality of the automobiles being manufactured there, and decided to work on a different idea — a stronger, faster, and sturdier vehicle. (p. 37)

Page 47

1. Most autos were handcrafted, making them extremely expensive. The Model T was one of the first cars made on an assembly line. This method of assembly sped up the production of automobiles. It also helped make the Model Ts more affordable for ordinary people to buy. (p. 37)

2. Assembly lines made it easier to build cars because each worker had only one or two tasks. They could do a lot more in one day than if they had to build the whole car. (p. 35)

Page 48

3. Answers may vary.

4. MACHINIST (p. 39)

5. Answers may vary.

6. Answers may vary.

7. Answers may vary.

Page 49

1. Answers may vary.

2. Answers may vary.

Page 50

3. It was a tough, sturdy car, big enough for the whole family, and it became very affordable. (p. 37)

4. Answers may vary.

Page 51

Answers may vary; however, student should show an understanding of how assembly lines work.

Page 54

Answers may vary. (p. 48–49)

Page 55

1. Answers may vary.

Page 56

2. Reasons might include: The *Olympic* (a *Titanic* sister ship) was also built by the same company but it had been sailing for a couple of years when the *Titanic* was completed (p. 45); the ship builders claimed it was safe (p. 46); it was designed by some of the most experienced and advanced engineers of that time. (p. 46)

Page 57

1. Answers may vary.

Page 58

2. The U.S. Senate investigation about the sinking led to new safety rules to prevent disasters like this from happening again. (p. 53)

3. Answers may vary.

4. Answers may vary.

5. STERN (p. 47)

6. Answers may vary.

7. Answers may vary.

8. Answers may vary.

Page 59

Answers may vary; however, student should show an understanding of how the night's events took place when the *Titanic* went down.

Page 64

Trench foot was a disease caused by the filth in the trenches during war. (p. 56)

Page 67

Make a Menu! Plan a week's worth of meals using Hoover's Food Administration guidelines of:

1. Student must list a meal that includes no wheat.

2. Student must list a meal that includes no meat.

3. Student must list a meal that includes no wheat.

4. Student must list a meal that includes no pork.

5. Student may list any meal; no restrictions.

6. Student must list a meal that includes no pork.

Page 68

7. STALEMATE (p. 59)

8. Answers may vary.

9. Answers may vary.

10. Answers may vary.

11. President Woodrow Wilson was finally forced to join the war after Germany tried to entice Mexico to declare war on the United States. A telegraph carrying this information from Berlin to Mexico was intercepted by secret British Navy intelligence. The United States declared war on Germany and was now officially a member of the Allied Powers. (p. 57)

12. Answers may vary.

Page 69

1. Doughboys (p. 59)

2. The *Lusitania* (p. 57)

3. The "Great War," "the War to End All Wars," and "the War in Europe." (p. 56)

4. Due to the racism of the time, they had to serve in segregated units, but nevertheless, many African American men served with distinction. (p. 59)

Page 70

5. For the first time, women could enlist in the military, with some working as army telephone operators and others performing clerical work for the Navy and Marines. As soon as the war was over, they were no longer eligible for military service, but women across the country had experienced all sorts of new freedoms and opportunities during the war. (p. 58–59)

6. Soldiers were massed in great numbers in training camps, in miserable living conditions on the battlefield, or in crowded troop ships. That meant the flu was easily passed among them and all around the world as these soldiers arrived at and left the war zones. (p. 62)

7. Answers may vary.

Page 71

Answers may vary; however, student should show an understanding of the day-to-day struggles either a soldier or person on the homefront would be subject to experience on account of the war.

Page 74

Prohibition banned people from selling and drinking alcohol. This did not keep people from drinking or selling alcohol, however! Secret nightclubs called speakeasies were abundant, with the alcohol being supplied by bootleggers, people who illegally made it. If anything, the fact that alcohol was illegal seemed to encourage people to drink it even more than before. (p. 66)

Page 75

1. Increased wages were making it easier for people to afford things like refrigerators, cars, and washing machines. (p. 67)

2. Answers may include: dancing the night away to the new sounds of jazz; watching silent movies; listening to the radio; playing and/or listening to/watching sports. (p. 67–68)

3. The popularity of jazz helped make an aspect of African American culture a part of everyday life for Americans of all races. (p. 47)

Page 76

4. Fashion changes caused women to start wearing clothing that only a decade earlier would have been unimaginable. In the 1910s, women wore floor-length dresses, but in the 1920s, women were wearing knee-length dresses. Hats went from elaborate styles adorned with feathers and flowers to relatively simple, smaller cloche styles. (p. 67)

5. JAZZ (p. 66)

6. Answers may vary.

7. Answers may vary.

8. Answers may vary.

9. Answers may vary.

10. Answers may vary.

11. Answers may vary.

Page 77

Map answers on page 71 of student book.

Page 78

1. Answers may vary.

2. One of the key differences between these incidents and previous acts of racial violence is that African Americans, many of whom were war veterans, organized a defense and fought back. (p. 71)

3. Small farms went under by the thousands as prices dropped and debt skyrocketed. One of the problems was that farmers had increased production for the war to help feed Europe. Once the war was over, however, this excess production was not necessary. It became hard for farmers to sell all their crops, and prices for farm products in general fell. (p. 69)

4. The Scopes trial (p. 70)

5. Because of the media coverage of the event, evolution was considered a valid scientific theory, and it now was okay to question the Bible and the biblical account of creation. The influence of this case is still felt today. By the 1960s, evolution was being taught in all public schools as an accepted fact. (p. 70)

Page 79

Answers may vary; however, student should show an understanding of the challenges that were taking place during the 1920s as discussed in this chapter. Examples may include: how to deal with the growing popularity of the KKK, how to handle people opposing Prohibition, the fear of communism, how to revive the farming community, evolution taking over the school system, racial tensions, etc.

Page 82

Answers may vary; however, student should show an understanding of how learning to wisely manage and spend money at a young age will have a positive effect on the rest of his or her life financially.

Page 83

1. Answers may vary.

Page 84

2. Answers may vary; however, student should show an understanding of what happened during the stock market crash of 1929 — investors either lost money selling stocks or what stock they still owned was worth much less than it had been. Because people had lost a lot of money and therefore cut spending, that hurt businesses who couldn't make money off sales. (p. 79)

3. If you own a share in a company, then you own a little bit of that company. Businesses sell shares because it gives them even more money than what they already make when they sell goods. Investors buy shares because if the company does really well, the stock prices will go up, and they will make money.

4. The average weekly salary after the war during the 1920s was around $25; before the war it would have been around half of that — $12.50. (p. 76)

5. Everyone said that there was no way to lose money because the stock market just kept going up and up. (p. 76–77)

6. $1,800 (reference p. 77)

Page 85

1. Chicago, Kansas City, and Minneapolis

2. San Francisco

3. New York; Philadelphia; Boston; and Washington, D.C

Page 86

4. Answers may vary.

5. Banks had been key to loaning people money to purchase stocks; when the market crashed, the banks lost a lot of money. Frightened people, who often showed up in crowds, demanded their savings and other funds. (p. 82)

6. A bull market is a favorable one and people tend to buy stocks. A bear market is when conditions are not favorable, and people tend to sell stock. (p. 82)

7. STOCKBROKER (p. 78)

8. Answers may vary.

9. Answers may vary.

10. Answers may vary.

11. Answers may vary.

Page 87

Answers may vary; however, student should show an understanding of the chaos caused by the stock market crash and how it impacted everyone from banks, businesses, and stock brokers to innocent bystanders.

Page 90

Answers may vary.

Page 92

1. Life was very hard for Americans during the Great Depression. By 1932, the unemployment was nearly at 25% — roughly 1 in 4 workers were without jobs. People were gathering by the thousands at local soup kitchens and bread lines so that they could have something to eat. Those who were working were making a lot less money than they had a few years earlier. (p. 86)

2. Banks were failing at record numbers. This caused people to be nervous about leaving money in a bank, and the result was similar to the panic selling that caused the stock market to crash. With banks, though, instead of panic selling, people would panic and pull all their money out of the bank. This was called a bank run because a lot of people would do it at the same time. (p. 86)

Page 93

1. East

Page 94

2. Answers may vary; however, student should show an understanding that the more connections you have, the less you would need to travel.

3. Hobos; they were homeless and illegally hopped on trains to travel for work. (p. 86)

4. Answers may vary; however, student should show an understanding of the difficulties being experienced at the time.

5. TOPSOIL (p. 89)

6. Answers may vary.

7. Answers may vary.

8. Answers may vary.

Page 95

Answers may vary; however, student should show an understanding of the following text taken from page 89 of the student book:

For the farmers living in the Dust Bowl regions, already affected by the Great Depression, the dust storms were devastating. There was no topsoil, no crop, and no way to pay the bank. Hundreds of thousands of people were homeless. Most of these families piled everything they had left into their vehicles and headed for the West Coast, looking for jobs. These Dust Bowl migrants became known as Okies or Arkies because they came from places like Oklahoma and Arkansas. Many settled in California, though life was no easier because there were simply not enough jobs for all of them in California either. Many ended up working for very low wages as farm hands and traveling from one farm job to another.

Page 98

The Great Depression was still affecting the United States, and that was the focus for most people. Though many Americans felt sorry for people in war-torn countries, the majority did not want to drag the country into a conflict they believed had little to do with them. Memories of the destruction and loss of life from World War I were still fresh for many people. (p. 98)

The attack on Pearl Harbor shocked and angered Americans. Many Americans feared that the next attack would be on the mainland. Before Pearl Harbor, Americans were divided about whether they should be involved in the war, but that wasn't the case anymore. People banded together to fight for our country. It truly was this war that ended the Great Depression, since the production of military supplies and weapons helped provide jobs for people. All over the country, Americans prepared to defend our nation. (p. 99)

Page 99

1. Looking at the map, the student should understand that it would be especially terrifying due to the close proximity of the attack at Pearl Harbor to the mainland of the United States.

Page 100

2. No

3. American ships were reported torpedoed on the high seas between San Francisco and Honolulu. The Japanese Government launched an attack against Malaya. Japanese forces attacked Hong Kong, Guam, the Philippine Islands, Wake Island, and Midway Island.

4. During the intervening time, the Japanese government deliberately sought to deceive the United States by false statements and expressions of hope for continued peace.

5. The Congress

6. December 8, 1941

Page 103

Answers may vary; however, the student should show an understanding of the surprise that ensued on account of this attack. During the intervening time, the Japanese government deliberately sought to deceive the United States by false statements and expressions of hope for continued peace.

Page 104

1. A couple of Japanese Americans on the Hawaiian island of Ni'ihau helped a crashed Japanese pilot who participated in the attacks, though they did not know it at the time. Initially placed under guard by the islanders following radio reports of the attack, the pilot managed to convince the couple to help him and they took the guard hostage. The incident led to widespread distrust of Japanese Americans and would help precipitate a terrible injustice — the internment of these American citizens in camps for the duration of the war. (p. 101)

2. Answers may vary; however, student should provide logical reasons to support the stance taken.

3. REPARATIONS (p. 97)

4. Answers may vary.

5. Answers may vary.

6. Answers may vary.

Page 105

Answers may vary.

Page 110

Japan held thousands of miles of territory across the Pacific. (p. 106) America could not simply invade Japan to end the war. American forces would need to invade Japanese-held territory in the Pacific to establish air and naval bases. Without these bases, they could not supply planes, ships, and military personnel needed for such an attack. (p. 107)

Page 111

1. Since America's two main allies during the war — Britain and the USSR — were under direct attack, it was decided that it would be better to relieve the pressure on them by defeating Germany and then everyone could focus their attention on Japan. (p. 106)

Page 112

2. Messerschmitt

3. Heinkel

4. Junkers

5. Focke-Wulf

Page 113

1. Answers may vary; however, student should understand that conquering the islands in this systematic way helped break up Japan's "protective ring" while keeping America's forces strong. See the following text from page 107:

   Japan's conquests had provided the country with a protective ring of a couple thousand miles. To invade Japan, the Americans would need to invade a series of islands. That way, the newly conquered island could serve as a base of supply for the next island that was invaded and so on. Without these bases, they could not supply planes, ships, and military personnel needed for such an attack. Following this method, the military could work its way close enough to

Japan to stage an invasion, as well as to bomb targets in the country.

2. By the end of the battle, the Americans had lost more ships than the Japanese, but the Japanese lost two important carriers and had to stop their invasion. It was technically an American defeat, but it hurt Japan worse. (p. 108)

3. America decisively defeated the Japanese navy in the Battle of Midway. In this battle, four more Japanese aircraft carriers were sunk, and over 3,000 Japanese military personnel were lost, including many experienced pilots and technicians. Between the Battles of Midway and the Coral Sea, the Japanese navy had suffered irreparable damage. (p. 108)

Page 114

4. AIRCRAFT CARRIER (p. 108)

5. Answers may vary.

6. Answers may vary.

7. Answers may vary.

Page 115

Answers may vary.

Page 118

Answers may vary.

Page 119

Answers may vary.

Page 120

1. Answers may vary.

2. The Nazis had murdered millions of people, including Jews, Gypsies, the physically and mentally disabled, as well as political prisoners, at special camps. (p. 119-120)

3. Answers should reflect the following text: Europe was severely affected by the years of warfare and bombing. There were food shortages and many of the governments were in a state of chaos. The full extent of the Nazis' cruelty was also revealed. The Nazis had murdered millions of people, including Jews, Gypsies, the physically and mentally disabled, as

well as political prisoners, at special camps. Many of the remaining survivors were in Germany. They needed immediate medical care, but they also had no homes to return to. Other civilians were also homeless and had nowhere to go. In fact, seven to eight million Europeans were homeless after the war had ended. (p. 119–120)

4. The military was predicting that this invasion would take at least another year and would lead to at least 400,000 more American deaths — nearly the number already lost since Pearl Harbor — and millions of Japanese civilian casualties. (p. 120)

Because of these casualty estimates, Harry S. Truman decided to use a top-secret weapon to end the war earlier. In August 1945, he ordered two atomic bombs dropped on Japan at Hiroshima and Nagasaki. (p. 120)

Page 121

1. Guam
2. New Hebrides
3. Aleutian
4. Okinawa
5. a. Soviet Union; b. China; c. Australia; d. Papua New Guinea; e. Fiji; f. Aleutian Islands

Page 122

6. PARATROOPER (p.117)
7. Answers may vary.
8. Answers may vary.
9. Answers may vary.

Page 123

Answers may vary; however, student should show an understanding of the important role this "fake army" played in the success of the allied invasion of Normandy on D-Day to confuse the Germans.

Page 126

1. It was not quite as unusual for women to work during the Great Depression as it had been earlier in the 20th century, but it was still not very common. During World War I, women had worked in wartime factories, but even more women did during World War II. These women did tasks, like welding, that had previously been reserved for men. (p. 126)

2. BOND (p. 126)
3. Answers may vary.
4. Answers may vary.
5. Answers may vary.

Page 128

1. By the end of the war, over 10,000,000 American men had been drafted into the armed forces. (p. 126)

2. Tanks, landing crafts, airplanes, machine guns, bombs, and ships. (p. 126)

3. Women turned out by the thousands to replace the men who had been drafted or enlisted. (p. 126)

4. Just like in World War I, many African Americans found better jobs in war factories and enlisted to serve their country. Because of the racism of the time, African American soldiers served in segregated units and at first were not assigned combat positions. Nevertheless, as the war continued, the military began to allow more African American soldiers to serve in combat positions. (p. 127)

Page 130

1. The United States wanted to make sure that there was enough food, gasoline, and rubber for the military overseas. That led to rationing in the United States. Each person received a booklet each month, which included stamps for rationed food items, such as meat, sugar, and coffee. People had to have these official stamps to buy these goods. Even fabrics like nylons and silk were rationed. (p. 128)

2. People participated in scrap metal drives. All of those ships and tanks the United States was building required a lot of metal, and people were encouraged to donate any metal they had to the war effort. People turned in car bumpers, fences, tractors, sculptures, and pots and pans in scrap metal drives. (p. 129)

3. Forming and equipping a large army was expensive. The government raised money by

selling bonds. People could buy bonds and then get their money back and a little more when they redeemed them years later. People were encouraged to help the war efforts through buying war bonds. (p. 128)

4. Answers may vary; however, student should show an understanding of the purpose the victory gardens served — to help ensure there were no food shortages during the war.

Page 133

Answers may vary; however, student should relay an understanding of the undesirable living conditions as described in the text below:

Within days of Pearl Harbor, suspicion fell upon them, though two-thirds of them were born in the United States. By 1942, nearly 120,000 Japanese Americans were moved to internment camps. These were primitive, overcrowded camps in remote areas of California, Idaho, Utah, Arizona, Wyoming, Colorado, and Arkansas. Despite no proof of them being disloyal to the country, Japanese Americans, including many American citizens, were forced to leave their homes, businesses, and jobs. Many stayed in the camps for years, and when they were released, they had no homes or jobs. (p. 129)

Page 136

After World War II had ended, the Soviet Union took advantage of the war-weakened countries of Eastern Europe and moved to install communist satellite governments that were under their control. America did not like this, and one of the reasons so much aid was provided to Western Europe was to strengthen these countries against the threat of Soviet and communist expansion. The tension got so bad between the United States and the Soviet Union that the two became engaged in the Cold War with each other. This conflict lasted from 1947 until 1991. It was called a "cold war" because the countries never directly fought each other. (p. 137)

Page 137

1. American soldiers were part of the occupation of both Germany and Japan. The American military also oversaw trials of people who had committed war crimes against civilians and soldiers. (p. 136)

Page 138

2. America provided loans to Western European countries to rebuild as part of the Marshall Plan. Named after George C. Marshall, Truman's Secretary of State and Roosevelt's Chief of Staff during the war, this plan provided food, fuel, equipment, and investments to European countries to prevent starvation and also to help them revive their economies. (p. 136)

3. Americans opposed the alliance because of the Soviet Union's communism, mistreatment of its citizens, and previous alliance with Nazi Germany. (p. 136–137)

4. It was called a "cold war" because the countries never directly fought each other. One reason they never engaged in combat is people were sick of war. The world was just coming out of the most devastating war it had ever experienced, and there had already been two deadly, destructive world wars within a span of thirty years. The atomic bombings of Japan added another fear. (p. 137)

Page 139

1. The best way to stop the Soviet Union was to prevent it from getting a foothold in another country, according to this theory. So, when the Soviets would try to start funding, equipping, and training rebels in a foreign country with the hopes of setting up a communist government, the United States would intervene and fund, equip, and train anti-communist forces. (p. 138)

Page 140

2. Eisenhower supported the policy of containment and also promised an end to the Korean War. Within a few months of his inauguration and after nearly three years of fighting, an armistice was signed. This was not an official peace treaty, but it ended the fighting in July 1953. Korea was to remain divided, with a communist north and a non-communist south. (p. 139)

3. In 1948, the Soviet Union blockaded the

Allied-controlled parts of Berlin. They hoped it would make the Allies leave. Instead, Americans used cargo planes to bring in needed supplies. This began the Berlin Airlift — an amazing feat as a fleet of American cargo planes would bring over 1,500 tons of food each day to feed the almost 2 million at risk in the city. (p. 142)

4. OCCUPATION (p. 139)

5. Answers may vary.

6. Answers may vary.

7. Answers may vary.

Page 141

Answers may vary.

Page 144

Answers may vary, but should include such things as the prosperity, growing car industry, diners and drive-ins, music scene, television, clothing styles, and games. (p. 146–147)

Page 145

1. It became a status symbol to own a car. Americans loved their cars, and most families had one! The American culture became more and more centered around the automobile industry. Soon, drive-in movies and drive-in diners were the rage. A family would drive up to a drive-in diner, where a waitress on roller skates would come to take their orders. Road trip vacations across the country became popular. Road systems began to improve to accommodate these new motorists. (p. 146)

2. Families gathered around their television sets to watch their favorite shows. Shows like *Leave it to Beaver, Davy Crockett, I Love Lucy*, and westerns like *Gunsmoke* and *The Lone Ranger* were well loved by everyone. At this time in American history, manly chivalry and dedication to family were highly admired and were the main theme of many shows and movies of this era. Many of the famous male actors and singers from this time period were World War II veterans and had just come home from defending their country's freedom. (p. 146–147)

Page 146

3. *Ben-Hur, The Ten Commandments, Singing in the Rain,* and *Oklahoma*. (p. 147)

4. Answers may vary; however, answer should reflect the following text:

Clothing styles during the 1950s reflected the culture of the time. Fashion styles were fun and, for the most part, still relatively modest. Teenage girls wore blue jeans rolled up to show their white "bobby socks" and black and white saddle shoes. "Poodle" skirts were also popular. These full skirts with a poodle appliqué were often worn over fluffy crinoline slips, coupled with a fitted top, curled ponytail, bobby socks, and saddle shoes. Boys were clean-cut and wore blue jeans along with white t-shirts and super-shiny penny loafers. It was considered "hip" to place a shiny new penny in the "slot" of the penny loafers. (p. 147)

Page 147

1. The tension of the Cold War frightened people. As the conflict with the Soviet Union became sharper and communism spread to other countries, Americans truly began to fear that communists were in the United States and actively plotting the overthrow of the U.S. government. (p. 148)

Page 148

2. It was a time when Americans feared that communists were in the United States and actively plotting the overthrow of the U.S. government. (p. 148)

3. Student should show an understanding of the abuse of power this man used to manipulate people under his authority.

Joseph McCarthy helped fan the flames of the Red Scare. Anyone who angered him could be condemned as a communist, regardless of whether the charge was true. Soon, even people who had never been communist sympathizers were being unfairly called communists. People were reluctant to criticize him for fear that they would be labeled communists too. (p. 148–149)

4. Though the Civil War had ended slavery almost

a hundred years before, African Americans still did not have the same rights and freedoms as white Americans. They were made to attend different schools, drink from separate water fountains, and even sit in the most unwanted seats at a movie theater. (p. 149)

5. SYMPATHIZER (p. 148)

6. Answers may vary.

7. Answers may vary.

8. Answers may vary.

9. Answers may vary.

Page 149

Answers may vary; however, student's answer and chosen locations should reflect the map on pages 150–151 in the student book.

Page 154

1. This organization was intended to help work toward progress and peace in developing countries. The Peace Corps sent volunteers around the world to work in agriculture, health care, education, and community organization. The Peace Corps was a way to combat what Kennedy saw as "the common enemies of man: tyranny, poverty, disease, and war itself." but it was also a way to prevent the Soviet Union from gaining a foothold in these poor countries, as well. (p. 156–157)

2. FRENCH INDOCHINA (p. 159)

3. Answers may vary.

4. Answers may vary.

5. Answers may vary.

Page 155

1. Answers may vary.

2. Answers may vary.

Page 156

3. By placing missiles on the communist island of Cuba, a little over one hundred miles from the United States, the Soviet Union was creating a direct threat to the safety of Americans. The missiles could have easily reached targets over most of the continental United States. It had

seemed that an actual war was now inevitable before the Soviets agreed to remove the missiles. (p. 161)

4. Where the 50s had been a time of traditional American life, with strong family ties and relatively high morals, the 60s were a time of experimentation and great turmoil for the United States. (p. 156)

Page 157

1. Communism claims to eliminate social classes and oppression. In reality, it empowers dictators to oppress people. (p. 160)

Page 158

2. The U.S. mission in Vietnam was the same as it had been in Korea: to stop the spread of communism. (p. 160)

3. Answers may vary.

4. Part of being a good steward is taking care of what is entrusted to you. You also need to take care of your stuff by keeping it clean and maintained. You should also not be greedy about what you own — you should try to share it with others when you can. (p. 164)

Page 159

Answers may vary.

Page 162

Answers may vary, but might include Kevlar, ATMs, pacemakers, and space exploration. (p. 172)

Page 164

1. HIPPIE (p. 169)

2. Answers may vary.

3. Answers may vary.

4. Answers may vary.

5. Answers may vary.

6. Answers may vary.

7. Answers may vary.

8. The "hippie" style of clothing and hair reflected the "peace" and "love" way of thinking and was very different from what people wore in

the 1950s. Both young men and women let their hair grow long. Flowers, beads, and other "natural" elements were brought into their clothing and hairstyles, as well. Not everyone was a "hippie," though. There were those who still dressed more traditionally, but skirt lines were considerably higher than the previous decade of the 1950s. (p. 169)

Page 165

1. Answers may include: progress in the fields of medicine and science, progress in space technology and travel, progress in women's rights movement, moral changes/bad progress in the school systems. (p. 166–167)

2. Like in World War I and World War II, a draft was started to increase the size of the military to fight the war in Vietnam. There had been some very limited opposition to these earlier drafts, but most people served when drafted. That was not the case during the Vietnam War. A draft was started for it, and even though nowhere near as many men were drafted, there was strong resistance to the draft by many people. Some found ways around the draft by pretending to be sick or by finding work in occupations that were exempt. Still others fled across the border to Canada to escape the draft. (p. 169)

Page 166

3. The Supreme Court banned school-sponsored prayer and Bible readings in public school. According to these rulings, it was unconstitutional for schools to have mandatory prayer or Bible readings. Before these rulings, it was a common occurrence for the school day to start with prayer. After these Supreme Court rulings, teachers and other school employees could get in trouble for doing such a thing. (p. 167)

4. Answers may vary.

Page 167

Answers may vary.

Page 170

Answers may vary.

Page 171

1. When African American students enrolled in all white schools and colleges, they were treated cruelly by those who opposed desegregation. (p. 180)

2. Seeing an empty seat in the middle of the bus, Ms. Parks sat down. The bus driver ordered her to give up her seat to a white man who wanted it. Rosa Parks politely declined and told them that there were other seats farther back. She quietly and politely refused to oblige no matter how much the driver yelled at her to move. As she later explained, she was tired of being pushed around. The driver became so angry that he called the police, and Ms. Parks was arrested. (p. 176–177)

Page 172

3. Dr. Martin Luther King Jr. was one of the Montgomery Bus Boycott organizers who came to the forefront as a civil rights leader. Dr. King was an advocate of peaceful protest. (p. 178)

4. African Americans rioted in cities across the country. It seemed that the rage, which had been suppressed for so long, had finally boiled over. Riots also broke out across the country following Dr. King's assassination. (p. 179)

5. INTEGRATION (p. 179)

6. Answers may vary.

7. Answers may vary.

8. Answers may vary.

Page 173

1. Jim Crow laws had been passed in the South to legalize segregation. (p. 176) They were laws designed to prevent equality. (p. 180)

Page 174

2. Dr. King was an advocate of peaceful protest. Malcolm X preached that the blacks should rise up and fight for their freedoms. (p. 178)

3. Freedom Summer was organized in 1964 to register African Americans in Mississippi to vote, a right long denied to many of them.

4. Answers may vary; however, student should

relay an understanding that God never intended for us to be "separate" or segregated, but to love one another as He created us to be — one race and one blood.

Page 175

Answers may vary; however, student should show an understanding as to why this event took place – to outlaw segregation on city buses. It was the first of many organized civil rights protests to come.

Page 178

Answers may vary; however, student should provide knowledgeable reasons in support of the decision made.

Page 179

1. Answers may vary.

Page 180

2. Unlike past conflicts, Americans at home witnessed the violence of war through TV news reports in their living rooms. (p. 186)

3. Some of the protests included young men burning their draft cards or even the American flag; other protests grew violent. By the early 1970s, many Americans were as tired of the protests as they were of the war. (p. 187)

4. Nixon promised to end the war; however, he increased American involvement with a secret bombing. Anti-war protesters were upset that Nixon had gone back on his promise, but they were even more angry that he had increased U.S. involvement without telling the American public. (p. 188)

5. Vietnam (p. 188)

6. Billy Graham was a Southern Baptist preacher who was part of a movement known as the evangelical movement. (Evangelical Christians believe in the mission to spread Christianity and the message of Jesus around the world. They also believe that Christians should affect the culture around them.) (p. 189)

Page 181

1. Answers may include, but are not limited to: fitness and exercise — aerobics, jogging, and exercise videos; eating healthy and natural foods; disco music; tall platform shoes; tight, vibrant clothing; bell-bottom pants; roller skates and roller derby; colorful cars; etc.

Page 182

2. They worked towards the opportunity to seek a higher education (such as college); to receive equal wages compared with men in the workplace; for the right to have careers of their own. Women were limited to working in certain jobs such as secretaries, teachers, nurses, and clerks through most of the 20th century. However, by advocating for equal rights, women were able to become doctors, lawyers, and CEOs — along with the careers they previously were allowed to choose. (p. 189)

3. The American Indian Movement (AIM) fought for equal rights and treatment of Native Americans. Many Native American communities faced racism, police harassment, unemployment, and poor housing, along with other problems like drug abuse and alcoholism. They also wanted the U.S. government to better honor their treaties. (p. 189)

4. EMBASSY (p. 188)

5. Answers may vary.

6. Answers may vary.

7. Answers may vary.

Page 183

Answers may vary.

Page 186

Spiro Agnew was President Nixon's vice president. Vice President Spiro Agnew was charged with criminal behavior in the various political offices that he had held. (p. 197)

Page 187

1. Spiro Agnew resigned from the office of vice president on October 10, 1973. Gerald Ford became the vice president in his place, so when President Nixon resigned months later, Ford became the 38th president of the United States of America without ever being elected for executive office. (p. 197)

Page 188

2. Because of his involvement with the Watergate break-in and his methods of trying to cover up the crime, President Nixon was facing impeachment. (p.196) Although Congress tried to impeach Nixon, he decided to resign from office on August 9, 1974, before the impeachment could take place. (p. 197)

3. Years of protest, the violence of the Vietnam War, and the Watergate Scandal caused many Americans to grow suspicious of and less confident in the U.S. presidency. (p.198)

Page 189

1. Foreign oil providers issued an oil embargo against the United States because these countries did not like that the United States was helping Israel in its wars. The 1973 oil embargo caused huge shortages throughout the country. (p. 198)

2. Answers may vary, but might include keeping supplies of oil available not controlled by foreign countries. (p. 200)

Page 190

3. An economic recession is like a depression because the unemployment rate rises in both instances, but a depression is worse than a recession. The recession lasted from 1973 to 1975 in the United States. (p. 199)

4. Answers may vary.

5. PRICE CONTROLS (p. 199)

6. Answers may vary.

7. Answers may vary.

8. Answers may vary.

Page 191

Answers may vary; however, student should show an understanding of the negative effects the oil crisis played in the economy of the United States. The price of gas also drove up the price of goods, the economy worsened, and Americans had to adjust their lifestyles to meet these new limitations.

Page 196

President Reagan's governing method was called "Reaganomics." Reaganomics called for reduced government spending, reduced federal income tax, reduced government regulation, and reduced inflation. Although Reaganomics did help improve the American economy, some have noted that his policies helped richer Americans and business more than average citizens. (p. 207)

Page 197

1. Muslim extremists were holding more than 50 American embassy workers hostage with the intent to overthrow the reigning shah, or king, of Iran. (p. 206)

Page 198

2. Answers should reflect the following text: The United States and the Soviet Union continued to build up their nuclear stockpiles, with the promise that if one country struck first, the other would immediately strike back. The result of such a nuclear fight would have completely destroyed both countries and the surrounding areas, changing the global climate for centuries to come. This is known as mutually assured destruction, or MAD, which prevented either side from ever using their nuclear weapons. (p. 206)

3. Answers may include but are not limited to: reduced government spending; reduced federal

income tax; reduced government regulation; and reduced inflation. (p. 207)

Page 199

1. Washington, Montana, North Dakota, Kansas, Iowa, Arkansas, Louisiana, Michigan, Indiana, North Carolina, Pennsylvania, New Jersey, Delaware, Maryland. (p. 210–211)

2. Answers may vary.

3. NASA was prepared to send people into space again in 1986. However, seven people — six astronauts and one schoolteacher — died seconds after takeoff when the shuttle (the *Challenger*) exploded. (p. 209)

4. Sending people into space was a point of pride and accomplishment, but seeing the *Challenger* explode in mid-air revealed how dangerous space travel can be. (p. 209)

Page 200

5. SUBSIDY (p. 207)

6. Answers may vary.

7. Answers may vary.

8. Answers may vary.

Page 201

Answers may vary.

Page 204

The three-branch system allows for the separation of powers. When the colonists rebelled against the English government and created a new country, they wanted to make sure the government would not be too powerful. It is important to have a strong leader, like a president, but they did not want him to become like the king of England. That's why they established the three branches of government and the separation of powers. (p. 218)

Page 205

1. Answers may vary; however, student should show a good understanding as to why people wanted the wall torn down during this time as described on pages 216–217 of the student book.

Page 206

2. The legislative branch makes laws. This branch is made up of Congress, Senate, and the House of Representatives. The executive branch carries out, or executes, laws. This branch is made up of the president, the vice president, and the president's cabinet. The judicial branch interprets and evaluates laws. This branch is made up of the Supreme Court and other federal courts. (p. 218–219)

3. The Constitution gives each branch different duties and powers. One branch cannot function without the other. Checks and balances also allow the branches to make sure the others are acting constitutionally, or according to the laws of the Constitution. (p. 219)

4. Answers may vary; however, student should understand that by doing it this way, each branch of government keeps the other branches from becoming too powerful.

5. ADVISER (p. 217)

6. Answers may vary.

7. Answers may vary.

8. Answers may vary.

Page 207

Answers may vary on 1–10.

Page 208

Answers may vary on 11–15.

Page 209

Answers may vary; however, student should relay an understanding of the mass celebrations that broke out at the Berlin Wall when East Germany announced that people were free to travel between East and West Germany.

Page 212

By the 1990s, many more people owned their own computers. The World Wide Web became accessible to the public in 1991. Before, it was only available to the government and the military. (p. 227)

Page 213

1. Answers may vary.

Page 214

2. Saddam Hussein was a dictator who ruled the Middle Eastern country of Iraq. Iraq invaded Kuwait because it believed Kuwait was drilling oil from Iraq's territory. Also, Iraq owed Kuwait money from a previous war. Iraq asked Kuwait to forgive the debt, but Kuwait refused. For these reasons and more, Iraq decided to take over Kuwait. (p. 228)

3. Answer should reflect the following text: The United States told Iraq that it had to leave Kuwait or go to war. The countries tried to solve the situation peacefully, but Iraq would not leave. President Bush and the United States led a group of 28 countries to stand up against Saddam Hussein by blocking trade with Iraq. The United Nations approved using force if Iraq did not get out of Kuwait. Saddam Hussein did not listen, and on January 16, 1991, the United States Armed Forces led an attack against Iraq. (p. 228)

4. Thanks to the advances in technology, weapons were much better than in any war before. Technology didn't just change how the war was fought. It also changed how people saw the war. (p. 229)

Page 215

1. C is the best answer.

Page 216

2. As you can see from the maps on these pages, access to internet service is still limited in some areas due to the geography or remoteness. (p. 231)

3. SOFTWARE (p. 227)

4. Answers may vary.

5. Answers may vary.

6. Answers may vary.

Page 217

Answers may vary; however, student should show an understanding as to why the United States got

involved in the war. We have learned about the evil dictators who tried to take over the world during World War II. These rulers have to be stopped, and this was the situation at hand. (reference p. 228)

Page 220

Although Clinton had many ideas for reform, conservative Republicans who were still in Congress opposed many of his ideas. The main reason given is because of his stance and push towards bigger government. (p. 236)

Page 221

1. In 1990, NASA set the Hubble Space Telescope into orbit. Unlike the *Challenger*, the Hubble Space Telescope was launched without astronauts. This amazing piece of equipment circles the earth, taking pictures of outer space. These pictures allow scientists to see into space better than ever before. (p. 237–238)

Page 222

2. President Clinton believed in bigger government. (p. 236)

3. If you consider how much of our nation and the world depends on computers, you can imagine what a disaster it would be if they all shut down at the same time. The electric grids would stop providing electricity, there would be no more telephone service, and our nation's ability to protect itself would be highly affected. (p. 239)

Page 223

1. Answers may vary.

2. Answers may vary.

Page 224

3. COMPUTER PROGRAMMER (p. 239)

4. Answers may vary.

5. Answers may vary.

6. Answers may vary.

Page 225

Answers may vary; however, students should show an understanding as to what Y2K was and the panic that ensued across the world because of it.

Page 228

Answers may vary; however, student should provide knowledgeable reasons to support the decision made.

Page 229

1. Answers may vary; however, answer should reflect the portions of text taken from the student book below:

   The election was too close to call in Florida in 2000. In fact, the vote was so close that Florida was required by state law to do a recount of the popular vote. Bush had the lead, but only by a few hundred votes. This proves that every vote counts (p. 249).

2. Answers may vary.

Page 230

3. Al Gore and George W. Bush (p. 248)

4. Answers may vary, but may include that the state of Florida had to recount its votes and that the electoral vote did not show the popular vote. (p. 249)

5. BALLOT (p. 249)

6. Answers may vary.

7. Answers may vary.

8. Answers may vary.

Page 231

1–7 in no particular order (p. 248): 1. California, 2. Texas, 3. Illinois, 4. Ohio, 5. Pennsylvania, 6. New York, 7. Florida

8. 210

Page 232

9–15 (p. 248): 9. Montana, 10. Wyoming, 11. South Dakota, 12. Delaware, 13. Vermont, 14. North Dakota, 15. Alaska

16. No; 270 electoral votes are needed to win (p. 248). Added to the electoral votes of the largest states, this only equals 231.

17. 11; 270 electoral votes are needed to win (p. 248). If you add up the 11 states with the largest electoral votes, you come up with 270.

18. Answers may vary.

Page 233

Answers may vary; however, student should understand that without the electoral college, about five heavily populated states would decide the presidency in every single election. (p. 254)

Page 238

Following the 9/11 attacks, patriotism was extremely high. All over the country, thousands of people came together to pay respect to Americans who had died in the tragedy. American flags adorned cars, trucks, and houses, and many people had patriotic signs on their lawns. (p. 257)

Page 239

1. Members of an extremist Islamic group called Al-Qaeda hijacked four commercial airliners, which were full of passengers, to destroy prominent American government and commerce buildings. (p. 256)

Page 240

2. Answers may vary, but might include the following: The people drew closer together and became more patriotic. The government established new security systems, including a new government department, the Department of Homeland Security. America also planned to strike back in the "War of Terror." America started to go after Iraq as they were suspected of harboring terrorists and weapons of mass destruction.

3. Answers may vary but should reflect the following text:

   President Bush established a new government department, the Department of Homeland Security. Their goal is to heighten security measures in order to protect our country against attacks. The United States National Guard, Coast Guard, and Customs and Border Protection are just a few of the departments that work with Homeland Security. Security checks in airports, especially, were much more thorough than before 9/11. Higher airport security also mandated that only passengers could go past a certain point. The laws concerning passports are now much more strict, as well. (p. 258)

4. He was captured at gunpoint and taken into custody and eventually tried and executed. (p. 258)

Page 241

1. New Orleans

2. Florida

Page 242

3. Answers may vary; however, some possible answers (not found in the student book) include: having a good evacuation plan; having access to clean food, water, and air; knowing how to dispose of waste; having ways of communication during and after the storm; how to deal with the lack of electricity a storm like this would cause; clean-up safety; etc.

4. Answers may vary; however, student should provide knowledgeable solutions to the problems he or she listed in the previous question and answer.

5. TERRORIST (p. 258)

6. Answers may vary.

7. Answers may vary.

8. Answers may vary.

Page 243

Answers may vary.

Page 246

Many of the issues surrounding the 2016 election are still being determined today. Among them are access to healthcare, immigration laws, and the fight against ISIS and terrorism. (p. 268)

Page 247

1. Answers may vary, but might include the growing concerns over war in the Middle East and the economic problems (p. 266).

Page 248

2. People had bought houses they could not afford because banks had been willing to give them risky loans. When they couldn't pay their loans back, people lost their homes, and banks lost their money. (p. 266)

3. He promised to end the war in Iraq and also promised a change in the economy. (p. 66)

4. It became the law, punishable by fine, that every American has health care insurance. (p. 267)

Page 249

1. Answers may vary.

2. Answers may vary.

3. Answers may vary.

Page 250

4. HEALTH INSURANCE (p. 267)

5. Answers may vary.

6. Answers may vary.

7. Answers may vary.

Page 251

Answers may vary; however, student should show an understanding of the devastation this natural disaster caused to New Orleans, killing 1,836 people and creating damage estimated at over $81 billion in the affected areas.

Page 254

Answers may vary; however, student should provide knowledgeable reasons to support the decision made, showing an understanding of how that particular branch of military works.

Page 255

1. Answers may vary.

Page 256

2. THE ARMY: is responsible for any military operations that take place on land. THE MARINE CORPS: is responsible for defending naval bases to support the Navy, developing tactics, techniques, and equipment, and other duties directed by the president. THE NAVY: is responsible for all of the military operations at sea. THE AIR FORCE: is responsible for the air. THE COAST GUARD: is responsible

for maritime safety, maritime security, and maritime stewardship.

3. Answers may vary; however, student should understand that by splitting the military up this way, it helps provide the U.S with a wider range of protection — air, sea, land, etc. — and also allows each of these branches to be more focused on each of their tasks versus if they were all clumped together. If this were the case, they would all have to worry about every aspect of every branch.

4. Answers may vary; however, student should understand that each branch tends to hold the similar, if not the same, core values. We all play on the same, team. Also, each branch tends to overlap another branch in some way. For example, the Marine Corps is a "bridge" between the Army and the Navy. Marines have also functioned as land-based combat and air forces in both Iraq and Afghanistan.

Page 257

1. Answers may vary, but should note the closeness to the country's leadership.

2. Answers may vary; however, student should understand that the reason entrance requirements for service academies are so difficult is so that the people being accepted are best prepared for the difficult tasks that will lay ahead of them. They need people who exemplify leadership, intelligence, and physical fitness.

Page 258

3. Answers may vary; however, student should provide knowledgeable ways to show honor and respect to veterans. Some examples we suggested in the book were to take some time to talk to and thank the veterans they know or to make them a Thank You card. (p. 279) Another idea was to find a cemetery to visit and pay respects, perhaps even helping put flowers on the graves of these veterans. (p. 284)

4. MARITIME (p. 279)

5. Answers may vary.

6. Answers may vary.

7. Answers may vary.

Page 259

Answers may vary; however, student should provide a knowledgeable answer as to the most important issue he or she thinks the country is facing during President Donald Trump's time in office and provide knowledgeable solutions to this problem. Some examples of the issues surrounding the 2016 election are given in the last paragraph of page 268 in the previous chapter. These include: access to healthcare, immigration laws, and the fight against ISIS and terrorism.

Review Answers

Page 271

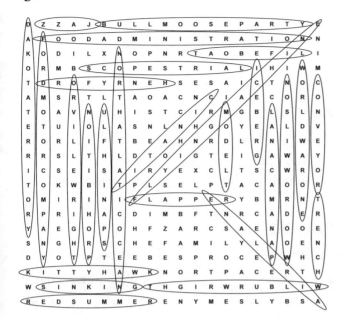

Page 273

1. Calvin Coolidge
2. Dust Bowl
3. Franklin D. Roosevelt
4. Great Depression
5. Herbert Hoover
6. Investment
7. New Deal
8. Stock Market
9. Ticker tape
10. Unemployment

Page 275

Across
1. USS *Arizona*
3. Pearl Harbor
5. Paratroopers
6. James Doolittle
8. War Bonds
11. Island Hopping
14. Double Victory
17. Douglas MacArthur
18. Imperial Japan
19. Marshall Islands
20. Victory
21. Hiroshima

Down
2. African American
4. Battle of Midway
7. Flying Fortress
9. Atomic Bomb
10. Interment Camps
12. Philippines
13. Nazi Germany
15. Code Talkers
16. Homefront

Page 276

1. h
2. g
3. f
4. a
5. e
6. c
7. i
8. b
9. d

Page 277

1. Route 66
2. Elvis Presley
3. *Leave It to Beaver*
4. Poodle Skirt
5. Sympathizer
6. Joseph McCarthy
7. Blacklisted
8. Segregation

Timeline Twisters!

1. 1962
2. 1960
3. 1953
4. 1952
5. 1968
6. 1969
7. 1954
8. 1962
9. 1964
10. 1971
11. 1972
12. 1973
13. 1974
14. 1976
15. 1980

Page 278

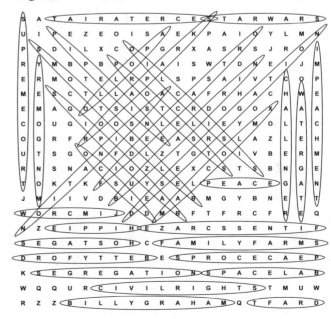

Page 279

1. Reagan
2. Berlin Wall
3. George H.W. Bush
4. Gen. Schwarzkopf
5. Clinton
6. Hubble
7. Gore
8. Bush
9. World Trade Center
10. Obama

Monumental!

1. Tomb of the Unknown Soldier
2. Arlington National Cemetery
3. Jefferson Memorial
4. World War II Memorial
5. Washington Monument
6. Lincoln Memorial
7. Vietnam Women Memorial
8. Vietnam Veterans Memorial Statue

Page 280

Answers: J, E, L, E, L, J, L, E

Page 281

1. Lyndon B. Johnson
2. Richard Nixon
3. Gerald Ford
4. George W. Bush
5. Barack Obama
6. Donald Trump
7. Jimmy Carter
8. Ronald Reagan
9. George H.W. Bush
10. Woodrow Wilson
11. Calvin Coolidge
12. Herbert Hoover
13. Franklin D. Roosevelt
14. Harry S. Truman
15. Dwight D. Eisenhower
16. Theodore Roosevelt

Page 282

1. WWI
2. Spanish-American War
3. WWII
4. WWI
5. Persian Gulf War
6. Korean War
7. Spanish-American War
8. Vietnam War
9. WWII
10. WWI

Quotable!

1. President Theodore Roosevelt
2. President William Taft
3. President Kennedy
4. President Franklin D. Roosevelt
5. Henry Ford

Page 283

1. Scopes Trial
2. Teaching evolution in public schools
3. Williams Jennings Bryan
4. Clarence Darrow

Pages 283–284

1. Bull Moose
2. *Titanic*
3. Henry Ford
4. Wright Brothers
5. *Lusitania*
6. Spanish Flu
7. Prohibition
8. Scopes Trial
9. Racial tension and communism
10. Stock market
11. Great Depression
12. Pearl Harbor
13. Japanese Americans
14. Japan
15. Europe
16. Nuremberg Trials
17. African Americans
18. Cold War
19. Atomic bombs
20. 1950s
21. Civil Rights
22. Cuban Missile Crisis
23. America
24. Prayer and Bible readings
25. Dr. Martin Luther King Jr.
26. Rosa Parks
27. Billy Graham

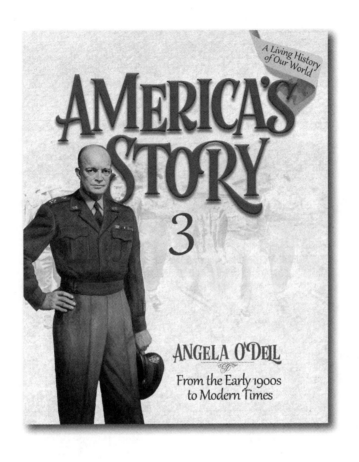

Glossary and Geographical Terms

for Use with

America's Story 3

Adviser: someone who gives advice

Aircraft Carrier: a ship that carries planes and is large enough for the planes to take off and land on the deck

Ballot: a ballot is how people cast their votes for candidates and issues; it can be a card or paper or on a machine

Bond: an investment in which the money will be paid back in full plus interest at a set time

Computer Programmer: someone who writes programs that a computer uses to operate

Embassy: the building where a diplomat and his or her staff work

French Indochina: a French colonial holding in southeast Asia in modern-day Vietnam, Cambodia, and Laos

Glider: an engine-less aircraft that moves by being carried by air currents

Health Insurance: insurance that pays for medical costs

Hippie: someone who rejected social and moral norms, especially in the 1960s

Integration: blacks and whites interacting together in the same neighborhoods, schools, and/or businesses

Jazz: a type of music developed by African Americans in New Orleans in the early 1900s

Machinist: a worker who makes or repairs parts with machine tools, such as lathes, milling machines, and grinders

Maritime: related to the sea

Monopoly: one company controls a market or good, which can lead to high prices

Occupation: when a military is stationed in a former enemy's land to maintain order

Paratrooper: a soldier who is trained to parachute into battle from an aircraft

Political Machine: organization controlled by a boss, who rewards supporters for loyalty

Price Controls: government efforts to prevent product prices from getting too high

Reparations: payments of money a country is required to make as an apology for past action

Software: the programs a computer uses to operate

Stalemate: a draw, neither side is going forward or moving back

Stern: the back part of the ship

Stockbroker: someone who buys and sells shares on the stock market for other people

Subsidy: money paid by the government to a business

Sympathizer: a person who supports an idea or organization

Terrorist: someone who uses violence to create fear for political purposes

Topsoil: the layer of soil that holds plant roots and most nutrients for plants

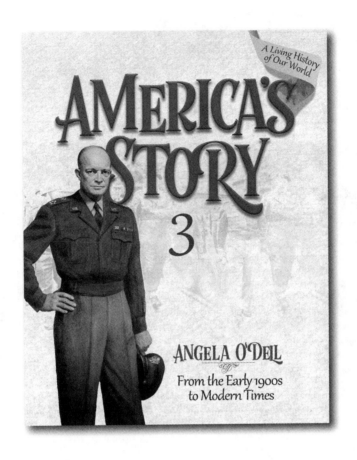

Special Projects

for Use with

America's Story 3

Welcome to our "American Landmarks" project! This optional activity helps you explore national, state, and/or local landmarks. The choice is yours!

The following pages contain journaling space for you to draw and write about different landmarks you learn about. If you are close enough to them, you can also pay them a visit!

You will work on 3 landmark pages. They can be national monuments related to topics we covered this year (like the Wright Brothers' National Memorial, Hoover Dam, the USS *Arizona* Memorial, or one of the national war memorials). They can be state monuments. They can also be local monuments or historical sites in your area. You can mix and match them or do all 3 from the same category.

For local monuments and sites, anything from local museums to battlefields to cemeteries to historic buildings would be great options. Your town may have a war monument you can visit. Your area might also host a local festival with a historic connection!

You can check the National Historic Landmarks site to learn about places in your state and the National Register of Historic Places or ideas on what to visit in your town or county.

In the journal pages, for each landmark, you will need an image of the landmark. You can draw it or cut out a photograph or print one from online or even add one you took yourself. Then fill in the history of this landmark and why it is famous. You'll also answer whether you have ever visited it and try to research some information about the area it is located.

Remember, even if you don't have a chance to complete the journaling activities, you can still try to visit local sites of historic interest and have conversations with your friends and family about what makes that site famous.

![American Landmark Project logo]

Landmark's Name _____   My Name _____

Landmark's History

_____

_____

_____

_____

_____

_____

_____

_____

Landmark Image

_____

_____

_____

_____

_____

_____

_____

_____

_____

_____

_____

_____

_____

_____

AMERICAN LANDMARK PROJECT

Landmark's Name _____   My Name _____

Landmark's History

_____
_____
_____
_____
_____
_____
_____
_____
_____

Landmark Image

_____
_____
_____
_____
_____
_____
_____
_____
_____
_____
_____
_____
_____
_____

Landmark's Name

My Name

Landmark's History

_____

_____

_____

_____

_____

_____

_____

_____

Landmark Image

_____

_____

_____

_____

_____

_____

_____

_____

_____

_____

_____

_____

_____

_____

_____

_____

_____

Learn the Presidents, Part 1 – Review

In *America's Story, Volume 2*, students learned the following list of presidents:

Memorize the first half of the presidents, including their names, dates, and numbers.

1. George Washington (1789–1797)
2. John Adams (1797–1801)
3. Thomas Jefferson (1801–1809)
4. James Madison (1809–1817)
5. James Monroe (1817–1825)
6. John Quincy Adams (1825–1829)
7. Andrew Jackson (1829–1837)
8. Martin Van Buren (1837–1841)
9. William Henry Harrison (1841)
10. John Tyler (1841–1845)
11. James K. Polk (1845–1849)
12. Zachary Taylor (1849–1850)
13. Millard Fillmore (1850–1853)
14. Franklin Pierce (1853–1857)
15. James Buchanan (1857–1861)
16. Abraham Lincoln (1861–1865)
17. Andrew Johnson (1865–1869)
18. Ulysses S. Grant (1869–1877)
19. Rutherford B. Hayes (1877–1881)
20. James A. Garfield (1881)
21. Chester Arthur (1881–1885)
22. Grover Cleveland (1885–1889)

Now for *Volume 3,* we will continue our **Learn the Presidents, Part 2:**

23. Benjamin Harrison (1889–1893)
24. Grover Cleveland (1893–1897)
25. William McKinley (1897–1901)
26. Theodore Roosevelt (1901–1909)
27. William Howard Taft (1909–1913)
28. Woodrow Wilson (1913–1921)
29. Warren Gamaliel Harding (1921–1923)
30. Calvin Coolidge (1923–1929)
31. Herbert Clark Hoover (1929–1933)
32. Franklin Delano Roosevelt (1933–1945)
33. Harry S. Truman (1945–1953)
34. Dwight David Eisenhower (1953–1961)
35. John Fitzgerald Kennedy (1961–1963)
36. Lyndon Baines Johnson (1963–1969)
37. Richard Milhous Nixon (1969–1974)
38. Gerald Rudolph Ford (1974–1977)
39. James Earl Carter Jr. (1977–1981)
40. Ronald Wilson Reagan (1981–1989)
41. George Herbert Walker Bush (1989–1993)
42. William Jefferson Clinton (1993–2001)
43. George Walker Bush (2001–2009)
44. Barack Hussein Obama (2009–2016)
45. Donald John Trump (2016–Present)

THANK YOU FOR YOUR SERVICE.

Fill in these short posters with information about the servicemen and women in your life! Be sure to ask them if it is okay first since some people find it difficult to talk about their time in the military, especially if they served in a war. If there is nobody for you to interview directly, ask your parents what they remember older relatives said about their time in the military. You might even be able to look at someone's military service records! I made an example for you to follow for this activity about my family's grandfather, Walter O'Dell.

Note: If your veteran has his or her decorations or medals, ask if you can see them. They each have a special meaning, which is fascinating to learn about.

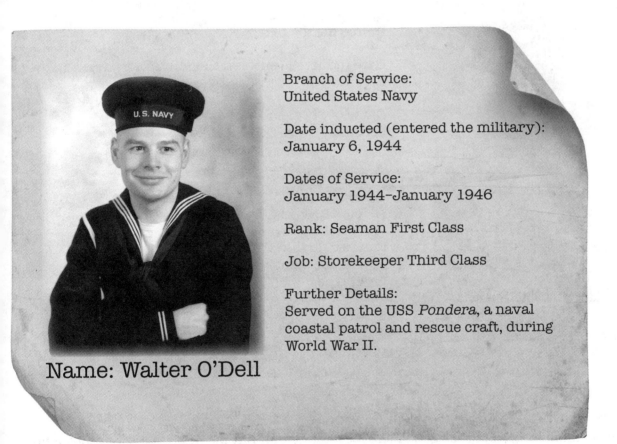

Branch of Service:
United States Navy

Date inducted (entered the military):
January 6, 1944

Dates of Service:
January 1944–January 1946

Rank: Seaman First Class

Job: Storekeeper Third Class

Further Details:
Served on the USS *Pondera*, a naval coastal patrol and rescue craft, during World War II.

Name: Walter O'Dell

Biography:

He was born February 6, 1922. He married his sweetheart, Arlene, in 1942 at the age of 20. By the time the photo was taken, he was the father of a little daughter and soon to be father of a little boy (my husband's dad). Walter and Arlene remained side by side in life until she passed away in late fall of 2015; they had been married 73 years. He followed one year later in November of 2016, at the age of 94. Both Grandpa and Grandma O'Dell are laid to rest in the Fort Snelling Military Cemetery (where my dad is also buried). They are dearly loved and missed.

If you can, ask the veterans for stories. They might tell you about their training, their close friends, or memorable experiences from their time in the military. Here's some information from my husband's great uncle Russ Rinkler.

Do you remember reading about the Philippines during World War II? General MacArthur promised he would return after the Japanese invaded, and he did. But the Philippines were not retaken overnight. It took several months. Russ was involved in the fight to take back the island of Luzon in early 1945. Below is an excerpt from a letter he wrote to his mother describing his arrival.

Name: Russ Rinkler

Branch of Service:
United States Army

Date inducted (entered the military):
February 17, 1941

Dates of Service:
February 1941-October 1945

Rank: Enlisted

Job: Regimental Casualty Clerk and Service Records

Further Details: Served in many key Pacific campaigns, including the Philippines.

Memories:

34 days ago I hit the beach in the biggest Philippine push. But hit isn't the word—actually, I waded from a sinking amphibious craft into water up to my neck and a few waves lifted me completely off the sandy ocean bottom. Exactly 35 minutes after our frontline troops waded ashore, I was standing on Philippine soil. . . .

[W]e went into the crowd of Filipinos [waiting for us]. There must have been about two hundred and every single one of them wanted to touch us and shake hands with us and thank us. A few of the old men cried and told us how they had waited for us every day for three years. We strolled into the woods where the women were, and it was there I broke down. They came up to see me, young and old, and dropped to their knees, sobbing and kissing my hand. One old woman pulled my hand to her face and held it there, while the tears rolled down her cheeks. I wonder what they thought when the tears began to flow out of my eyes. They were hungry, and in just a few moments I no longer had my two day supply of rations. So within myself I know I have the tiny distinction of being the first American soldier that many of the Filipinos saw in this invasion. It was more than a thrill, because the memory of those minutes will always reign supreme in my mind—it was an event that even the best journalists in the land could not amply describe.

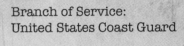

THANK YOU FOR YOUR SERVICE.

Don't forget that your "Thank You For Your Service!" pages can be about any veteran who served at any time. You can talk to an older relative who served in any of the wars covered in this book or someone who is currently enlisted in the military or recently left the service, like my nephew John. He served in the Coast Guard, and his wife Beth did, too. I really wanted to include a picture of Beth in her uniform, but unfortunately all her military pictures were lost in a computer crash.

Name: John Mark Tuohy

Branch of Service: United States Coast Guard

Date inducted (entered the military): 1998

Dates of Service: 2000–2014

Rank: E-7, Chief Boatswain's Mate

Job: Anti-Terrorism/Force Protection

Further Details: His work also included law enforcement in the North Pacific/Bering Sea/Gulf of Mexico, ship topsides maintenance, ship driving, personnel development/ training; he and his wife Elizabeth are now serving as the head pastoral team at a church in Talkeetna, Alaska.

Name: Elizabeth Tuohy

Branch of Service: United States Coast Guard

Date inducted (entered the military): 2000

Dates of Service: 2000-2004

Rank: E-4, Boatswain's Mate Third Class

Job: Boating Safety on the Great Lakes

Further Details: Her work also included rescue and survival systems, boat driving, and being part of the quick response force/ personnel surge that deployed to New York Harbor after the 9/11 attacks; she and her husband John are now serving as the head pastoral team at a church in Talkeetna, Alaska.

THANK YOU FOR YOUR SERVICE.

Fill in your own short posters with information about the servicemen and women in your life!

Branch of Service:

_____

Date inducted (entered the military):

_____

Dates of Service:

_____

Rank: _____

Job: _____

Further Details: _____

_____

_____

_____

Name:

Biography:

_____

_____

_____

_____

_____

_____

_____

Memories:

_____

_____

_____

_____

_____

_____

_____

_____

_____

_____

THANK YOU FOR YOUR SERVICE.

Fill in your own short posters with information about the servicemen and women in your life!

Branch of Service:

_____

Date inducted (entered the military):

_____

Dates of Service:

_____

Rank: _____

Job: _____

Further Details: _____

_____

_____

_____

Name:

Biography:

_____

_____

_____

_____

_____

_____

Memories:

_____

_____

_____

_____

_____

_____

_____

_____

_____

_____

THANK YOU FOR YOUR SERVICE.

Fill in your own short posters with information about the servicemen and women in your life!

Branch of Service:

_____

Date inducted (entered the military):

_____

Dates of Service:

_____

Rank: _____

Job: _____

Further Details: _____

_____

_____

_____

Name:

Biography:

_____

_____

_____

_____

_____

_____

_____

Memories:

_____

_____

_____

_____

_____

_____

_____

_____

_____

_____

THANK YOU FOR YOUR SERVICE.

Fill in your own short posters with information about the servicemen and women in your life!

Branch of Service:

_____

Date inducted (entered the military):

_____

Dates of Service:

_____

Rank: _____

Job: _____

Further Details: _____

_____

_____

_____

Name: _____

Biography:

_____

_____

_____

_____

_____

_____

Memories:

_____

_____

_____

_____

_____

_____

_____

_____

_____

_____

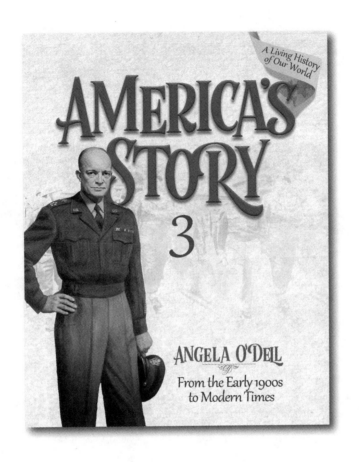

Timeline Activity Cards

for Use with

America's Story 3

The Wright Brothers
start experiments
at Kitty Hawk

October 1900

Theodore Roosevelt
re-elected president

November 1904

Titanic strikes
iceberg and sinks

April 14–15, 1912

Woodrow Wilson
re-elected president

November 1916

World War I ends

November 11, 1918

The famed U.S. Route 66 opens

November 1926

The 15-millionth & final
Model T assembled

May 26, 1927

Giant dust storms plague
areas of the Great Plains

1930–1940

Japanese attack Pearl
Harbor; U.S. joins WWII

December 7, 1941

U.S. forces "island-hopping" in Pacific

1942–1945

Allied D-Day
Invasion of France

June 1944

Atomic bomb dropped
on Hiroshima

August 6, 1945

U.S. supplies city in "Berlin
Airlift"

June 1948–May 1949

Dwight D. Eisenhower
elected president

November 1952

Rosa Parks arrested
for refusing to move
to back of a bus

December 1, 1955

NASA founded

July 1958

Cuban Missile Crisis

October 1962

Neil Armstrong of Apollo
11 mission walks on the
moon

July 20, 1969

Watergate break-in

June 17, 1972

1973 oil crisis

October 1973

Jimmy Carter
elected president

November 1976

Reagan re-elected president

November 1984

The Berlin Wall topples

November 1989

Persian Gulf War

January 16,1991–
February 28, 1991

Y2K computer scare

1999

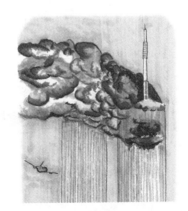

9/11 terrorist attack

September 11, 2001

President George W.
Bush re-elected

November 2004

Barack Obama
re-elected president

November 2012

Donald Trump
elected president

November 2016

Me in History!

_____

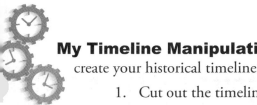

My Timeline Manipulative. To create your historical timeline:

1. Cut out the timeline strips.
2. Paste the strips together in chronological order.
3. Affix the strip to the wall, poster board, or surface where you can add significant people, places, and events where they occurred in time.

1980	1955	1930	1900	
			1905	
2005	1985	1960	1935	1915
2010	1990	1965	1940	1920
2015	1995	1970	1945	
2020	2000	1975	1950	

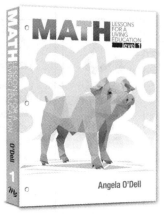
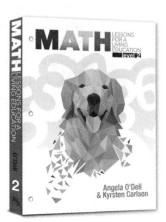
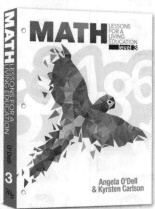

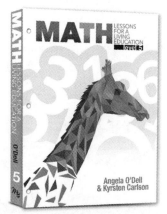

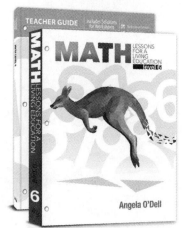

CHARLOTTE MASON INSPIRED
ELEMENTARY CURRICULUM THAT CONNECTS CHILDREN TO
AMERICA'S PAST... AND THEIR FUTURE!

Through this unique educational style, children develop comprehension through oral and written narration, and create memories through notebooking and hands-on crafts. This is not just facts and figures; this is living history for grades 3 through 6.

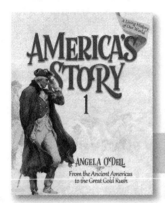

FROM THE ANCIENT AMERICAS TO THE GREAT GOLD RUSH

Part 1: Begins at the infancy of our country and travels through the founding of our great nation, catching glimpses of the men who would become known as the Founding Fathers.

America's Story Vol. 1
978-0-89051-979-0

Teacher Guide
978-0-89051-980-6

FROM THE CIVIL WAR TO THE INDUSTRIAL REVOLUTION

Part 2: Teaches students about the Civil War, the Wild West, and the Industrial Revolution.

America's Story Vol. 2
978-0-89051-981-3

Teacher Guide
978-0-89051-982-0

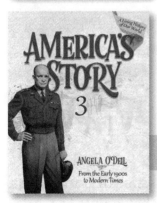

FROM THE EARLY 1900s TO OUR MODERN TIMES

Part 3: Carries the student from the turn of the 20th century through the early 2000s, seeing war through the eyes of the soldiers in journals and letters.

America's Story Vol. 3
978-0-89051-983-7

Teacher Guide
978-0-89051-984-4